THE
REFERENCE
SHELF

REPRESENTATIVE AMERICAN SPEECHES 1985–1986

edited by OWEN PETERSON
Professor, Department of Speech Communication
Louisiana State University

THE REFERENCE SHELF
Volume 58 Number 5

THE H. W. WILSON COMPANY
New York 1986

THE REFERENCE SHELF

The books in this series contain reprints of articles, excerpts from books, and addresses on current issues and social trends in the United States and other countries. There are six separately bound numbers in each volume, all of which are generally published in the same calendar year. One number is a collection of recent speeches; each of the others is devoted to a single subject and gives background information and discussion from various points of view, concluding with a comprehensive bibliography. Books in the series may be purchased individually or on subscription.

The Library of Congress has cataloged this serial title as follows:

Representative American speeches. 1937/38-
New York, H. W. Wilson Co.
v. 21 cm. (The Reference shelf)
Annual.
Indexes:
Author index: 1937/38-1959/60, with 1959/60;
1960/61-1969/70, with 1969/70; 1970/71-1979/80,
with 1979/80.
Editors: 1937/38-1958/59, A. C. Baird.—1959/60-69/70, L. Thonssen.—1970/71-1979/80, W. W. Braden.—1980/81- O. Peterson.
ISSN 0197-6923=Representative American speeches.
1. Speeches, addresses, etc., American. 2. Speeches, addresses, etc. I. Baird, Albert Craig, 1883- ed. II. Thonssen, Lester, 1904- ed. III. Braden, Waldo Warder, 1911- ed. IV. Peterson, Owen, 1924- ed. V. Series.
PS668.B3 815.5082 38-27962
MARC-S
Library of Congress [8503r85]rev4

Printed in the United States of America

CONTENTS

Academic Freedom or License?

Reaffirming the Past

Shaping the Future

Public Service and Private Support

PREFACE

One of the most important rhetorical developments in 1985–1986 was generated by the start of the race for the 1988 presidential nominations. Even before Ronald W. Reagan was sworn in for a second term in January 1985, members of both parties had begun jockeying for position in the next presidential sweepstakes. Competition was even more keen than usual, because 1988 will mark the first time in twenty years that an incumbent will not be contesting the election.

By most assessments, the impact of television on the political process, and on the journalism that reports on that process, is enormous. Since the 1950s, candidates have become increasingly aware of the influence of videoculture on election outcomes. Accordingly, the electoral contestants carefully weigh which speaking invitations to accept, which groups to address, and which issues to discuss. Timing is important: the candidate seeks to avoid both over- and underexposure, to ensure that his campaign is not "peaking" too early, and to prevent the kinds of gaffes that, because of wide media coverage, have effectively dashed the hopes of candidates in the past.

One major continuing concern often expressed by thoughtful observers is whether television's undeniable power in elections is beneficial or detrimental to the democratic political process. Rushworth M. Kidder, addressing the question "Do 'mediagenic' candidates make good leaders?" in the *Christian Science Monitor* (June 12, 1985, p. 12), cited several commentators:

> "My greatest concern about national campaigns," says ABC's [Peter] Jennings, "is that we will elect people in the future who are extremely adept at organizing their arguments and their campaigns for TV, but who are vastly less well-informed on the issues." James W. Carey, dean of the School of Communication at the University of Illinois, puts it another way. The "telegenic" candidate, he says, is "one who substitutes personality for ideology" but who may not be able to pass along his triumphs to his successors. And since the bias of so much of network television is toward amusement, says New York University's Neil Postman, all personalities channeled through television "appear inevitably to be packaged as a form of entertainment."

A second, and also continuing, major political concern is the tremendous cost of running for office and the resulting influence of Political Action Committees (PACs). According to Common Cause, the bipartisan citizens' lobbying group, in the past ten years PAC contributions to congressional candidates have skyrocketed from $12.5 million to more than $100 million in 1984. At the presidential level, conservative PACs spent a total of $15.8 million promoting Reagan's 1984 reelection, while liberal PACs spent $800,000 in support of Walter Mondale. In 1985, the Supreme Court struck a blow against attempts to restrict the influence of PACs by ruling that the First Amendment protects unlimited campaign expenditures by such committees.

Beside the political scene, two other areas of significant developments in rhetorical terms during 1985-86 were the reemergence of student activism on college and university campuses and the efforts of feminists to regroup and reinvigorate the women's movement.

Student protests, reminiscent of those of the 1960s, occurred at many colleges and universities, seeming to herald a reawakening of social concern among young people. Most often the issues were apartheid and campus recruiting by the Central Intelligence Agency. Several hundred students on campuses around the country were arrested or detained for demonstrating, occupying campus buildings, and violating regulations.

Interest in the women's movement, less apparent since the defeat of the Equal Rights Amendment, temporarily revived with the 1984 nomination of Geraldine Ferraro for vice president. In July 1985, the National Organization of Women elected as its leader a former NOW president, Eleanor Smeal, whose campaign platform called for greater activism, higher visibility, and a more militant stance against the growing conservatism of the country. This platform, along with appeals by well-known feminists for a more dynamic and aggressive approach to women's issues, seemed to mark a change of pace in the women's movement.

The current volume of *Representative American Speeches* includes addresses on several continuing issues related to foreign and domestic policy, civil rights, technology, and communications, as well as on several new and emerging problems. Of particular interest in 1985-1986 was the debate over the interpretation of the Constitution, the challenge to colleges and universities by a group concerned with accuracy in teaching, and a growing concern over liability litigation and our dependence on technology.

In preparing the collection, I rely heavily on the assistance, cooperation, and encouragement of many people. This year I particularly would like to express appreciation to Dann Brown, Susan Borque, Virginia Conrad, Patricia Garcia, and Jean Jackson. As usual, my colleagues at Louisiana State University provided me with support and useful advice. I thank Waldo W. Braden, Stephen L. Cooper, Gresdna Doty, Stephen Eisenbraun, Mary Frances Hopkins, Harold Mixon, and Jim Traynham.

I appreciate the help of many others who have supplied me with speeches and additional information. I wish to thank Cindy Fox Aisen, Randolph C. Arndt, Sam Becker, Jack Davies, Lamar Downtain, Terry Eastland, Kenneth Gladish, Robert Haakenson, Janet A. Hall, Richard L. Holzhausen, William R. Jenkins, Jordan E. Kurland, Wono Lee, Pat Matuka, Hannah Olanoff, Helaine Patterson, Stephen C. Schlesinger, Annette N. Shelby, Peter Tapke, John Thomas, Doug Thornburg, Artie Trash, Frank J. Williams, Harlington Wood, Jr., Molly Yard, and the Rockford Institute.

OWEN PETERSON

Baton Rouge, Louisiana
May 19, 1986

THE UNITED NATIONS AT 40

SPEECH ON THE 40TH ANNIVERSARY OF THE UNITED NATIONS[1]

RONALD W. REAGAN[2]

"Not even New York had seen anything quite like it before. Presidents, prime ministers, kings, and potentates from the four corners of the globe in town for the United Nations' 40th anniversary celebration strained city services, hotels, champagne stocks and, at times, tempers. There wasn't a $2,700-a-night suite left at the Waldorf-Astoria" (*U.S. News and World Report*, November 11, 1985, p. 29). Attending the 10-day event were 35 heads of state, 8 vice presidents, 33 prime ministers, 43 special envoys, and 1 deputy prime minister.

President Ronald Reagan of the United States, the first to address the General Assembly commemorative observance, spoke to a packed chamber at 10:00 AM on October 24, 1985. Although the speakers had been asked to limit their remarks to fifteen minutes, Reagan—like many others—exceeded the time limit, speaking for 29 minutes. His speech was broadcast on all three major U.S. television networks.

In the address to the General Assembly, as in talks with the allies, Reagan focused on a single theme: Soviet expansionism worsens the climate of superpower relations, making it hard to reach agreements in other fields. Sources said the original draft of the speech, written by speechwriter Kenneth Khachigian in collaboration with senior White House speechwriter Ben Elliott and communications director Patrick J. Buchanan, had a harder edge than the final version approved by Reagan (Lou Cannon, *Washington Post*, October 23, 1985, p. A16).

The speech was described as "combative" (Bernard Weinraub, *New York Times*, October 27, 1985, p. 1E), "a provocative sermon, glorifying the U.S. record while denouncing the Soviet record and the communist system" (James Reston, *New York Times*, October 27, 1985, p. E23), and "a good stiff dose of Ronald Reagan" (*Washington Post* editorial, October 25, 1985, p. A26). In *U.S. News and World Report* the address was termed "one of the President's sternest lectures to the Soviet Union," which nonetheless "was delivered in a tone of good will and with diplomatic words unlike the 'evil empire' imagery that he once employed" (November 4, 1985, p. 27).

Response to President Reagan's speech was, at best, mixed. *U.S. News and World Report* said he "drew mostly polite applause" (November 4, 1985, p. 27). The *New York Times* noted that Reagan was "not interrupted by applause . . . in contrast to last year, when his address to the United Nations spoke of the need to reach an arms agreement" (October 25,

[1]Delivered to the United Nations General Assembly in New York at 10:00 A.M. on October 24, 1985.
[2]For biographical note, see Appendix.

1985, p. 1). Noting with surprise that Reagan had spoken to the United Nations more times than any other American president (this was his fourth address), the *Times* of London (October 17, 1985, p. 17) summarized journalistic response to the speech as follows:

> The early impression was that he had rather a mixed response. The problem was not the delivery—Reagan was as polished and vigorous as ever—but the content. . . . Conservative senators praised it and the *Wall Street Journal* hailed it as a "declamatory masterpiece." But the *New York Times* described it as "a sermon likely to have no effect on anyone save the converted. . . . On the whole, the allies found the speech a little one-sided and simplistic.

President Reagan's speech: Forty years ago, the world awoke daring to believe hatred's unyielding grip had finally been broken—daring to believe the torch of peace would be protected in liberty's firm grasp.

Forty years ago, the world yearned to dream again innocent dreams, to believe in ideals with innocent trust. Dreams of trust are worthy, but in these 40 years too many dreams have been shattered, too many promises have been broken, too many lives have been lost. The painful truth is that the use of violence to take, to exercise, and to preserve power remains a persistent reality in much of the world.

The vision of the U.N. Charter—to spare succeeding generations this scourge of war—remains real. It still stirs our souls and warms our hearts. But it also demands of us a realism that is rock-hard, clear-eyed, steady and sure—a realism that understands the nations of the United Nations are not united.

I come before you this morning preoccupied with peace, with ensuring that the differences between some of us not be permitted to degenerate into open conflict. And I come offering for my own country a new commitment, a fresh start.

On this U.N. anniversary, we acknowledge its successes: the decisive action during the Korean War; negotiation of the Non-Proliferation Treaty; strong support for decolonization; and the laudable achievements by the U.N. High Commissioner for Refugees.

Nor must we close our eyes to this organization's disappointments: its failure to deal with real security issues, the total inversion of morality in the infamous Zionism-is-racism resolution, the politicization of too many agencies, the misuse of too many resources.

The U.N. is a political institution and politics requires compromise. We recognize that. But let us remember—from those first days, one guiding star was supposed to light our path toward the U.N. vision of peace and progress—the star of freedom.

What kind of people will we be 40 years from today? May we answer—free people, worthy of freedom, and firm in the conviction that freedom is not the sole prerogative of a chosen few, but the universal right of all God's children.

This is the Universal Declaration of Human Rights set forth in 1948. And this is the affirming flame the United States has held high to a watching world. We champion freedom not only because it is practical and beneficial, but because it is morally right and just.

Free people, whose governments rest upon the consent of the governed, do not wage war on their neighbors. Free people, blessed by economic opportunity, and protected by laws that respect the dignity of the individual, are not driven toward the domination of others.

We readily acknowledge that the United States is far from perfect. Yet we have endeavored earnestly to carry out our responsibilities to the Charter these past 40 years, and we take national pride in our contributions to peace:

We take pride in 40 years of helping avert a new world war and pride in our alliances that protect and preserve us and our friends from aggression. We take pride in the Camp David agreements and our efforts for peace in the Middle East rooted in resolutions 242 and 338; in supporting Pakistan, target of outside intimidation; in assisting El Salvador's struggle to carry forward its democratic revolution; in answering the appeal of our Caribbean friends in Grenada; in seeing Grenada's representative here today, voting the will of its own people. And we take pride in our proposals to reduce the weapons of war.

We submit this history as evidence of our sincerity of purpose. But today it is more important to speak to you about what my country proposes to do, in these closing years of the 20th century, to bring about a safer, a more peaceful, a more civilized world.

Let us begin with candor—with words that rest on plain and simple facts. The differences between America and the Soviet Union are deep and abiding.

The United States is a democratic nation. Here the people rule. We build no walls to keep them in, nor organize any system of police to keep them mute. We occupy no country. The only land abroad we occupy is beneath the graves where our heroes rest. What is called the West is a voluntary association of free nations, all of whom fiercely value their independence and their sovereignty. And as deeply as we cherish our beliefs, we do not seek to compel others to share them.

When we enjoy these vast freedoms as we do, it is difficult for us to understand the restrictions of dictatorships which seek to control each institution and every facet of people's lives, the expression of their beliefs, their movements, and their contacts with the outside world. It is difficult for us to understand the ideological premise that force is an acceptable way to expand a political system.

We Americans do not accept that any government has the right to command and order the lives of its people, that any nation has an historic right to use force to export its ideology. This belief—regarding the nature of man and the limitations of government—is at the core of our deep and abiding differences with the Soviet Union, differences that put us into natural conflict—and competition—with one another.

We would welcome enthusiastically a true competition of ideas, welcome a competition of economic strength and scientific and artistic creativity, and, yes, welcome a competition for the good will of the world's people. But we cannot accommodate ourselves to the use of force and subversion to consolidate and expand the reach of totalitarianism.

When Mr. Gorbachev and I meet in Geneva next month, I look to a fresh start in the relationship of our two nations. We can and should meet in the spirit that we can deal with our differences peacefully. That is what we expect.

The only way to resolve differences is to understand them. We must have candid and complete discussions of where dangers exist and where peace is being disrupted. Make no mistake: our policy of open and vigorous competition rests on a realistic view of the world. Therefore, at Geneva, we must review the reasons for the current level of mistrust.

For example, in 1972 the international community negotiated in good faith a ban on biological and toxin weapons; in 1975 we negotiated the Helsinki accords on human rights and freedoms; and during the decade just past, the United States and the Soviet Union negotiated several agreements on strategic weapons. Yet, we feel it will be necessary at Geneva to discuss with the Soviet Union what we believe are their violations of a number of the provisions in all of these agreements. Indeed, this is why it is important that we have this opportunity to air our differences through face-to-face meetings—to let frank talk substitute for anger and tension.

The United States has never sought treaties merely to paper over differences. We continue to believe that a nuclear war is one that cannot be won and must never be fought. That is why we have sought, for nearly 10 years, still seek, and will discuss in Geneva radical, equitable, verifiable reductions in these vast arsenals of offensive nuclear weapons.

At the beginning of the latest round of the ongoing negotiations in Geneva, the Soviet Union presented a specific proposal involving numerical values. We are studying the Soviet counterproposal carefully. I believe that within their proposal there are seeds which we should nurture, and in the coming weeks we will seek to establish a genuine process of give-and-take.

The United States is also seeking to discuss with the Soviet Union in Geneva the vital relationship between offensive and defensive systems, including the possibility of moving toward a more stable and secure world in which defenses play a growing role.

The ballistic missile is the most awesome, threatening, and destructive weapon in the history of man. Thus, I welcome the interest of the new Soviet leadership in the reduction of offensive strategic forces. Ultimately, we must remove this menace—once and for all—from the face of this Earth.

Until that day, the United States seeks to escape the prison of mutual terror by research and testing that could, in time, enable us to neutralize the threat of these ballistic missiles and, ultimately, render them obsolete.

How is Moscow threatened—if the capitals of other nations are protected? We do not ask that the Soviet leaders—whose country has suffered so much from war—leave their people defenseless against foreign attack. Why then do they insist that we remain undefended? Who is threatened if Western research—and Soviet research that is itself well-advanced—should develop a non-nuclear system which would threaten not human beings, but only ballistic missiles?

Surely, the world will sleep more secure when these missiles have been rendered useless, militarily and politically, when the Sword of Damocles that has hung over our planet for too many decades is lifted by Western and Russian scientists working to shield their cities and their citizens and one day shut down space as an avenue for weapons of mass destruction.

If we are destined by history to compete, militarily, to keep the peace, then let us compete in systems that defend our societies rather than weapons which can destroy us both, and much of God's creation along with us.

Some 18 years ago, then-Premier Aleksei Kosygin was asked about a moratorium on the development of an anti-missile defense system. The official Soviet news agency, TASS, reported he replied with these words:

"I believe that defensive systems, which prevent attack, are not the cause of the arms race, but constitute a factor preventing the death of people. . . . Maybe an anti-missile system is more expensive than an offensive system, but it is designed not to kill people but to preserve human lives."

Preserving lives. No peace is more fundamental than that. Great obstacles lie ahead, but they should not deter us. Peace is God's commandment. Peace is the holy shadow cast by men treading on the path of virtue.

But just as we all know what peace *is*, we certainly know what peace is *not*.

Peace based on repression cannot be true peace and is secure only when individuals are free to direct their own governments.

Peace based on partition cannot be true peace. Put simply: nothing can justify the continuing and permanent division of the European continent. Walls of partition and distrust must give way to greater communication for an Open World. Before leaving for Geneva, I shall make major new proposals to achieve this goal.

Peace based on mutual fear cannot be true peace because staking our future on a precarious balance of terror is not good enough. The world needs a balance of safety.

Finally, a peace based on averting our eyes from trouble cannot be true peace. The consequences of conflict are every bit as tragic when the destruction is contained within one country.

Real peace is what we seek, and that is why today the United States is presenting an initiative that addresses what will be a central issue in Geneva—the resolution of regional conflicts in Africa, Asia, and Central America.

Our own position is clear: as the oldest nation of the New World, as the first anti-colonial power, the United States rejoiced when decolonization gave birth to so many new nations after World War II. We have always supported the right of the people of each nation to define their own destiny. We have given $300 billion since 1945 to help people of other countries. And we have tried to help friendly governments defend against aggression, subversion, and terror.

We have noted with great interest similar expressions of peaceful intent by leaders of the Soviet Union. I am not here to challenge the good faith of what they say. But isn't it important for us to weigh the record, as well?

—In Afghanistan, there are 118,000 Soviet troops prosecuting war against the Afghan people.

—In Cambodia, 140,000 Soviet-backed Vietnamese soldiers wage a war of occupation.

—In Ethiopia, 1,700 Soviet advisers are involved in military planning and support operations along with 2,500 Cuban combat troops.

—In Angola, 1,200 Soviet military advisers involved in planning and supervising combat operations, along with 35,000 Cuban troops.

—In Nicaragua, some 8,000 Soviet bloc and Cuban personnel, including about 3,500 military and secret police personnel.

All of these conflicts—some of them under way for a decade—originate in local disputes but they share a common characteristic: they are the consequence of an ideology imposed from without, dividing nations and creating regimes that are, almost from the day they take power, at war with their own people. And in each case, Marxism-Leninism's war with the people becomes war with their neighbors.

These wars are exacting a staggering human toll and threaten to spill across national boundaries and trigger dangerous confrontations. Where is it more appropriate than right here at the United Nations to call attention to Article 2 of our Charter which instructs members to refrain "from the threat or use of force against the territorial integrity or political independence of any state. . . . "?

During the past decade these wars played a large role in building suspicions and tensions in my country over the purpose of Soviet policy. This gives us an extra reason to address them seriously today.

Last year I proposed from this podium that the United States and Soviet Union hold discussions on some of these issues, and we have done so. But I believe these problems need more than talk.

For that reason, we are proposing, and are fully committed to support, a regional peace process that seeks progress on three levels:

First, we believe the starting point must be a process of negotiation among the warring parties in each country I've mentioned—which, in the case of Afghanistan, includes the Soviet Union. The form of these talks may and should vary, but negotiations—and an improvement of internal political conditions—are essential to achieving an end to violence, the withdrawal of foreign troops and national reconciliation.

There is a second level: once negotiations take hold and the parties directly involved are making real progress, representatives of the United States and the Soviet Union should sit down together. It is not for us to impose any solutions in this separate set of talks. Such solutions would not last. But the issue we should address is how best to support the ongoing talks among the warring parties. In some cases, it might well be appropriate to consider guarantees for any agreements already reached. But in every case the primary task is to promote this goal: verified elimination of the foreign military presence and restraint on the flow of outside arms.

Finally, if these first two steps are successful, we could move on to the third—welcoming each country back into the world economy so its citizens can share in the dynamic growth that other developing countries—countries that *are* at peace—enjoy. Despite past differences with these regimes, the United States would respond generously to their democratic reconciliation with their own people, their respect for human rights, and their return to the family of free nations.

Of course, until such time as these negotiations result in definitive progress, America's support for struggling democratic resistance forces must not and shall not cease.

This plan is bold. And it is realistic. It is not a substitute for existing peace-making efforts; it complements them. We are not trying to solve every conflict in every region of the globe, and we recognize that each conflict has its own character. Naturally other regional problems will require different approaches. But we believe that the recurrent pattern of conflict that we see in these five cases ought to be broken as soon as possible.

We must begin somewhere, so let us begin where there is great need and great hope. This will be a clear step forward to help people choose their future more freely. Moreover, this is an extraordinary opportunity for the Soviet side to make a contribution to regional peace which in turn can promote future dialogue and negotiations on other critical issues.

With hard work and imagination, there is no limit to what, working together, our nations can achieve. Gaining a peaceful resolution of these conflicts will open whole new vistas for peace and progress—the discovery that the promise of the future lies not in measures of military defense, or the control of weapons, but in the expansion of individual freedom and human rights.

Only when the human spirit can worship, create, and build, only when people are given a personal stake in determining their own destiny and benefitting from their own risks do societies become prosperous, progressive, dynamic, and free.

We need only open our eyes to the economic evidence all around us. Nations that deny their people opportunity—in Eastern Europe, Indochina, southern Africa, and Latin America—without exception are dropping further behind in the race for the future.

But where we see enlightened leaders who understand that economic freedom and personal incentive are key to development, we see economies striding forward: Singapore, Taiwan, and South Korea, India, Botswana, and China. These are among the current and emerging success stories because they have the courage to give economic incentives a chance.

Let us all heed the simple eloquence in Andrei Sakharov's Nobel Peace Prize message: "International trust, mutual understanding, disarmament and international security are inconceivable without an open society with freedom of information, freedom of conscience, the right to publish and the right to travel and choose the country in which one wishes to live."

At the core, this is an eternal truth. Freedom works. That is the promise of the Open World and awaits only our collective grasp. Forty years ago, hope came alive again for a world that hungered for hope. I believe fervently that hope is still alive.

The United States has spoken with candor and conviction today, but that does not lessen these strong feelings held by every

American: It's in the nature of Americans to hate war and its destructiveness. We would rather wage our struggle to rebuild and renew, not to tear down. We would rather fight against hunger, disease, and catastrophe. We would rather engage our adversaries in the battle of ideals and ideas for the future.

These principles emerge from the innate openness and good character of our people—and from our long struggle and sacrifice for our liberties and the liberties of others. Americans always yearn for peace. They have a passion for life. They carry in their hearts a deep capacity for reconciliation.

Last year at this General Assembly, I indicated there was every reason for the United States and the Soviet Union to shorten the distance between us. In Geneva—the first meeting between our heads of government in more than 6 years—Mr. Gorbachev and I will have that opportunity.

So, yes, let us go to Geneva with both sides committed to dialogue. Let both sides go committed to a world with fewer nuclear weapons—and some day with none. Let both sides go committed to walk together on a safer path into the 21st century and to lay the foundation for enduring peace.

It is time, indeed, to do more than just talk of a better world. It is time to act. And we will act when nations cease to try to impose their ways upon others. And we will act when they realize that we, for whom the achievement of freedom has come dear, will do what we must to preserve it from assault.

America is committed to the world, because so much of the world is inside America. After all, only a few miles from this very room is our Statue of Liberty, past which life began anew for millions—where the peoples from nearly every country in this hall joined to build these United States.

The blood of each nation courses through the American vein—and feeds the spirit that compels us to involve ourselves in the fate of this good Earth. It is the same spirit that warms our heart in concern to help ease the desperate hunger that grips proud people on the African continent.

It is the internationalist spirit that came together last month when our neighbor, Mexico, was struck suddenly by an earthquake. Even as the Mexican nation moved vigorously into action, there were heartwarming offers by other nations offering to help and glimpses of people working together, without concern for national self-interest or gain.

And if there was any meaning to salvage out of that tragedy, it was found one day in a huge mound of rubble that was once the Juarez Hospital in Mexico City.

A week after that terrible event and as another day of despair unfolded—a team of workers heard a faint sound coming somewhere from the heart of the crushed concrete and twisted steel. Hoping beyond hope, they quickly burrowed toward it.

As the late afternoon light faded, and racing against time, they found what they had heard—and the first of three baby girls—newborn infants—emerged to the safety of the rescue team.

Here is the scene through the eyes of one who was there. "Everyone was so quiet when they lowered that little baby down in a basket covered with blankets. The baby didn't make a sound, either. But the minute they put her in the Red Cross ambulance everybody just got up and cheered."

Well, amidst all that hopelessness and debris came a timely—and timeless—lesson for us all. We witnessed the miracle of life.

It is on this that I believe our nations can make a renewed commitment. The miracle of life is given by One greater than ourselves. But once given, each life is ours to nurture and preserve—to foster not only for today's world but for a better one to come.

There is no purpose more noble than for us to sustain and celebrate life in a turbulent world. That is what we must do now. We have no higher duty—no greater cause as humans. Life—and the preservation of freedom to live it in dignity—is what we are on this Earth to do.

Everything we work to achieve must seek that end so that some day our prime ministers, our premiers, our presidents and our general secretaries will talk not of war and peace—but only of peace.

We've had 40 years to begin. Let us not waste one more moment to give back to the world all that we can in return for this miracle of life.

NATIONAL PRIORITIES

AT STAKE IS "A VISION OF OUR COUNTRY"[1]

HENRY G. CISNEROS[2]

On March 10, 1986, Mayor Henry G. Cisneros of San Antonio, president of the National League of Cities, predicted in an address to a plenary meeting of the league that proposed cuts in federal aid to cities would amount to a "disastrous dismantling of federal-local partnerships" and would require imposition of "regressive" local taxes.

Mayor Cisneros presented his address to an audience of 3,500 city officials—a record turnout—attending the 1986 Congressional-City Conference. Cisneros, who has two master's degrees—one in urban and regional planning from Texas A & M University and the other in public administration from Harvard—and a Ph.D. in public administration from George Washington University, was well qualified to address the group. The son of Mexican immigrants, he served two terms as a councilman in San Antonio, the tenth-largest American city. Then in 1981, at the age of 34, he was elected the city's first Mexican-American mayor since 1842.

In 1985 Cisneros became president of the National League of Cities, a federation of 49 state leagues with 1,126 city members. The league develops and pursues a national municipal policy that seeks to meet the future needs of cities and help them solve critical problems affecting metropolitan areas. It also represents municipalities in dealings with Congress and federal agencies.

Mayor Cisneros began his speech to league members by noting that "representatives of America's cities have been gathering at this conference, in this very room, for over 15 years. If these walls could speak, they would tell a powerful story of America and of its city leaders." Over the years, he noted, regardless of the prevailing political climate, the delegates had come together as "city officials first, Republicans and Democrats second, liberals, conservatives somewhere else, but city officials first."

But this year, according to Cisneros, was different:

> This year all of us together face a new problem that none of those who sat in these chairs has faced before. It is a disastrous dismantling of the federal-local partnership. It is a meat-ax chopping of the domestic obligations of government. These are not in the category of threats or distant storm clouds, but the realities of the next 90 or 120 days. The mood—our response—must not be gloom, or timidity, or uncertainty, or hang-dog apologetics.

[1]Delivered to a plenary session of the National League of Cities in the International Ballroom of the Washington Hilton Hotel, Washington, D.C., at 2:00 P.M. on March 10, 1986.

[2]For biographical note, see Appendix.

We must be determined to stand up for what is right in the face of what I can only call disrespect: a disrespect for our cities, disrespect for the people who govern them, and disrespect for the people who live in them.

Cisneros then elaborated on how the proposed federal cuts would affect all American cities and every city official present. He repeatedly stressed the urgency of the issue and the need for a unified response to it. Then, in an unusual move, the mayor presented a list of the "ten toughest questions" that city officials are likely to encounter from congressional representatives while lobbying against the spending reductions; he also provided succinct answers to each query. He concluded by urging the officials to action, telling them, "A lot of how it comes out is up to you and what you do over the course of the next 24 hours."

John Herbers, writing in the *New York Times* (March 11, 1986, p. 13), reported that Cisneros received a standing ovation following the speech. The next day hundreds of mayors and city council members in the audience visited Capitol Hill in a "massive, organized lobbying effort aimed at persuading Congress not to sacrifice domestic spending in the fight against federal deficits" (Baton Rouge, Louisiana, *State Times*, March 11, 1986, p. 18).

Henry G. Cisneros's speech: Representatives of America's cities have been gathering at this conference, in this very room, for over 15 years. If these walls could speak, they would tell a powerful story of America and of its city leaders.

In these seats where you sit now have sat leaders of the big cities and of the small communities, from the Northeast and from the Midwest, and the South and the West, from all across America. Recounting the history of this conference would tell a story of the places that we love and the dramatic story of America's cities.

Over the last 15 years since this room has been used in this way every year, we have seen miraculous turnarounds: stories such as those of Baltimore and Boston, and Indianapolis and Cleveland. We've seen smaller communities that have succeeded and that have given us leaders to the national organization, like Scotland Neck, North Carolina, and Sunnyvale, California. Communities like Lincoln, Nebraska, and Lancaster, Pennsylvania, Lowell, Massachusetts, Topeka, Kansas, Nitro, West Virginia, and Vancouver, Washington.

We've seen cities that were sort of in the second rung of cities and now are national powers like Tampa and Seattle and Atlanta, Minneapolis, Denver and Houston and San Jose and the second largest city in the country now—Los Angeles. We see the same cities that were struggling work to forge new roles for themselves to completely convert their economies and perform in this new era. Cities like Akron, Fort Wayne, Fort Worth, Rochester, Beaumont, and Tucson.

All in all, what we have seen are the performances of the finest public officials in American life. The jobs that they have done have been masterful, tough, independent, resourceful, financially responsible, and competent. All across those years that they have been here, you have been here. Sometimes, it was to build new partnerships as in the early 1970s when in this room, this organization met to celebrate the passing of revenue sharing signed by President Nixon. The mood then was excited and exuberant, optimistic and appreciative of the respect extended by the federal government.

Sometimes we met in years when the mood was more one of commiseration over the black clouds that loomed on the horizon far away—as in the Carter years—when the theme was high inflation. Or, in the early years of the Reagan presidency when we heard the first language of the New Federalism. The mood then was anxious and cautious.

But always we have been city officials first, Republicans and Democrats second, liberals, conservatives somewhere else, but city officials first.

This year all of us together face a new problem that none of those who sat in these chairs has faced before. It is a disastrous dismantling of the federal-local partnership. It is a meat-ax chopping of the domestic obligations of government.

These are not in the category of threats or distant storm clouds, but the realities of the next 90 to 120 days. The mood, our response, must not be gloom, or timidity, or uncertainty, or hang-dog apologetics.

We must be determined to stand up for what is right in the face of what I can only call disrespect: a disrespect for our cities, disrespect for the people who govern them, and disrespect for the people who live in them.

Now, if you think that the word "disrespect" is too strong, then I don't know any other word that describes what is happening. "Miscommunication" or "misunderstanding" doesn't explain it. The only word that I can find that fits the bill is disrespect.

How else can one account for the fact that in 1980 urban programs were $69 billion in our nation's budget, while today they are $17 billion, a dramatic cut? Yet over that same period of time, the deficit has grown from $27 billion to $200 billion. Picture that for a minute: a deficit that has grown from $27 to $200 billion, our programs have gone from $69 billion to $17 billion, and it is we who are blamed for the deficit! It is just not true, and don't you believe it!

I'll tell you what is true, though. What is true is that the loopholes in the tax codes are up 8 percent, while housing programs are down 67 percent. What is true is that foreign aid is up 8 percent, but job training is down 16 percent. What is true is that defense is up 12 percent, but municipal wastewater grants are down 25 percent.

Where is the balance, where is the equal sacrifice, where is the fairness in that? People of our cities will lose—not because there is a deficit—but because of the way the rules of the game have been set by the administration and the Congress.

When the rules of the game are set in this way, when you increase defense by 12 percent, when you leave the entitlements untouched so that they grow by 8 percent, when there are no new revenue sources at all, and when you hold tax reform revenue neutral and still try to balance the budget on the Gramm-Rudman timeframe, there is no way that you can win in the ball game.

The fact of the matter is that the numbers don't work. The only course when the rules of the game are set that way is to dismantle the domestic side of government, which may in fact have been the intent of some of those in the Congress and the administration all along.

In 1981, we had what was called the Gramm-Latta tax cut. It cut taxes on upper incomes with the supposed knowledge that it would invigorate the economy so that we would have a balanced budget in a few short years. Instead, we ended up with the worst deficit in the history of our country: $200 billion. So we now have Gramm-Rudman, which is supposed to solve what Gramm-Latta didn't, by dismantling the domestic side of government.

You may have seen a listing of some of the programs that are slated to be eliminated. It is a long list, and it includes a whole host of programs such as EDA [Environmental Development Agency], programs related to senior citizens' housing, FHA [Federal Housing Administration], and the Small Business Administration and countless others. Many of you have said that you want to know what we stand for. Before this meeting is out, we hope to set before you a priority list that indicates what programs this organization is going to fight for, recognizing that we can't fight for them all. But even as we are losing programs, we are also losing the capacity to generate revenues because of what is happening on the other side of the discussion—not the spending side, not the budget side, but with tax reform.

Tax reform [legislation] involves some $400 billion of incentives and credits in the tax code, and right now there is a Berlin Wall, if you will, placed between a tax code that is intended to be revenue neutral and the budget cuts that are being made. You end up with some really unfair contrasts.

For example, accelerated depreciation for office buildings went up from $10 billion in 1984 to $15 billion in 1986 in the tax code, while CDBG [Community Development Block Grant] was slated for a 32 percent reduction on the budget side.

Special capital gains treatment for timber went up by 150 percent in the tax code, while low-income housing will be down 67 percent in the budget.

Corporate tax breaks and subsidies are running at $140 billion in the tax code, while general revenue sharing will be cut out, aced out 100 percent in the budget.

The purchase price of a corporate plane can be recouped entirely through tax credits and deductions in the tax code, while city mass transit monies will be down 31 percent in the budget.

Again, where is the equality of sacrifice when we leave the tax code alone with some $400 billion and make all the cutting that needs to be made on the budget side?

But if that were not enough, tax reform goes even further and goes to the heart of the ability of cities to finance the self-reliance that is intended.

Of course the attack on state and local tax deductibility is one of those. We must remember that before there was a federal income tax, there were state and local taxes. These taxes already existed before there was a federal tax, and when the federal tax came into existence, it recognized the fact that people were paying state and local taxes.

So don't allow ourselves to be "walked into" the logic that says that we are just one other lobby group on the question of the tax code. Unlike other incentives built into the tax code to encourage some kind of spending or buying activity on the part of the American public, this is a fundamentally different thing.

The same thing is true of tax-exempt bonds. We've gotten ourselves into a situation where the enormity exists right now that the federal government mandates us to clean water, but calls the bonds that we'll need to do sewage treatment plants nonessential. That's the craziness, if you will, of this present situation, and so when I use the word "disrespect," that's exactly what I mean. There is no other way to describe it except as disrespect that is thoughtless and will result in years of damage.

The shape of our governmental system for 15 years is going to be set in the next 180 days, and I honestly don't believe that we can allow the dismantling of such a system that has been so productive: the breakup of working relationships that have been put together on a bipartisan fashion year in and year out, the closing of day-care centers, the termination of housing initiatives, the closing of senior citizen nutrition centers, the reduction of manpower training centers.

I honestly believe that you don't deserve to be portrayed as the inept managers who cut, slashed and chopped people programs because you didn't know how to manage. But that's the picture that will be facing urban America in another 180 days. No matter what size of city you come from, you have got to see that the homeless, the poor, and the old will not be going to the oak-panelled committee rooms in the Rayburn House Office Building to make their case. They're not going to be going to take their case to the white-gloved gentility of the West Wing of the White House. They are not going to penetrate the upper office suites of HUD [Housing and Urban Development] or the Treasury Department.

But they will be at your council offices. They will be at your offices at City Hall. And they will be even at your house.

You are the ones that are going to have to cut the parks in your community because there is no more revenue sharing. You are the ones that are going to have to cut day-care because there is no more community services block grant. You are the ones that are going to have to cut job training because there is no more Job Training Partnership Act.

You are the ones that are going to have to cut housing programs because CDBG has been reduced. You are the ones that are going to have to let sewer moratoria run a risk in your community because the Clean Water Act monies have been eliminated. You are the ones that are going to have to let traffic become congested because transportation programs are reduced.

And you are going to be the ones who raise taxes, because in 1986 the federal government decided to get out of the business of domestic America.

I've sensed some reluctance on the part of some of you over the course of the last days and weeks, some ambivalence, a sense even on the part of some that says, "I care about this program but not that program, and I'm here to work on mine and I'll make my arrangement with my congressmen, and as soon as we cut our deal then we'll sort of break away from the rest of the organization."

I understand some of that sense, because I come from a region where it is very difficult to articulate the kind of message that I'm trying to convey to you today. But this is one of those cases, ladies and gentlemen, where if we don't hang together, then we'll hang separately.

This is a time when we need to address some questions of attitude even before we get into tactics. I say one of the first things we need to address together and understand together is that there is no need to apologize because you run cities.

There is no need to apologize because you are sworn to uphold a city charter. It is an honorable place in our system; the cities of America are where 80 percent of the people of this country live. The cities of America are where the essential dynamics of modern American life occurs.

When the cure for cancer is found in this country, it is going to be found in the hospital of a great American city. When new ideas of government are advanced, it's in the neighborhood movements of American cities and towns. When new forms of art are advanced, it's in the galleries that exist in the cities. When new books and ideas in literature are contributed, it's in the university complexes that exist in your cities and towns.

All in all, the cities of America are important to this country, and as a result the city governments of America are important.

When people stop and think every night as they go to sleep, whether there is going to be somebody that they can depend on if their spouse should be walking across the bedroom floor and collapses of a heart attack, it's not some esoteric argument at that stage. It's a question of whether they can pick up the telephone and find that emergency medical service on the other end of that line that can get there in a reasonable span of time.

Or as one sleeps at night and worries about crime and burglary problems in the neighborhood, is there a police officer on hand that the city government put in place?

One sends one's children off to school in the morning in the knowledge that they are walking on sidewalks, through traffic signalization systems, on decent streets where the traffic flows safely, that the city made possible.

Even as they leave for their jobs, often it's to jobs in a restaurant or a retail center adjacent to something that the city government help put in place.

The point I'm making is simply that you have absolutely nothing to apologize for in fighting for these programs, nor for standing up for the place of cities in the American system of government.

This is not just another lobby group. The truth of the matter is that not one of you in this room will make one more penny next year in terms of what the charter salary is in your city, because you have fought to save CDBG.

This is not like someone who gets a bonus in their salary or who gets stock savings or stock options if they are successful in running their cities better. All you're trying to do is advocate for a place for people in the American system.

So there is no need to be defensive; in fact, we have a very good offense. Think about the business of running cities as defense and offense. Defense means protecting our cities against these kinds of incursions, whether they be budgetary or tax reform. On the other hand we have an offense which means what we do with our own capability in our respective towns.

We have one hell of an offense. We have an offense that includes Charley Royer and what he has managed to do to make Seattle an international city by developing that port capability and marketing that city. We have an offense that includes Bill Hudnut and what he's managed to do in Indianapolis, rebuilding that downtown and bringing back an older industrial city, and what Kathy Whitmire has done in Houston—despite the fact that the city is ravaged by the decline of oil and gas prices.

We have an offense that includes Mayor Schaefer in Baltimore and what he has been able to do with an old port city, or Buck Rinehart, mayor of Columbus, Ohio, and his unique relationships with the university there, and Bob Bolen in Fort Worth. And in the small communities, places like Lowell, Lancaster, and

Fort Wayne, there are countless examples of people who have been competent and self-reliant. There is nothing to apologize for on that scale.

But at the same time, when we're called upon to play defense, we have a defense as well. It begins with the priorities on the national agenda for the nation's cities.

Top of the list: General Revenue Sharing reenactment, and after that, other priority program reenactments: Community Development Block Grants, Urban Development Action Grants, environmental programs, transportation programs and the housing assistance programs.

Our priority is to try also to educate our people about the Gramm-Rudman-Hollings process, and so that is listed as a priority for this year. Other priorities include: tax reform, tax expenditures (which is that $400 billion that I described earlier that's available, but at the moment not being used for deficit reduction), federal mandates (which require that we clean water, but give us no revenues to clean it), and the liability insurance issues. Stated in one succinct format, these are the priorities of the National League of Cities in 1986.

In preparation for testimony recently, Mayor Voinovich and I asked the staff to prepare the 10 toughest questions that we were likely to encounter. We have reproduced those questions and some answers for your use in meetings with your congressmen and senators.

Question 1: Isn't it hypocritical for you to express concern about the federal deficit and then to oppose Gramm-Rudman because it will cut city programs?

No. Gramm-Rudman substitutes non-elected officials to make critical budget priority decisions affecting our taxpayers in place of the accountability and responsibility on the part of people who are elected to make those decisions. Gramm-Rudman is not fair. It applies to only 13 percent of the budget. That portion could be cut out 100 percent, and the budget would still not be balanced. Congress and the administration need to adopt fair and balanced deficit reduction budgets. The NLC board has adopted a budget priority statement that would reduce the deficit, but without increasing your property taxes or cutting your services.

Question 2: Aren't you really calling for a tax increase?

No. Tax reform would lead to increased revenues to reduce the deficit. The federal budget included federal tax subsidies, benefits and loopholes totalling more than $500 billion next year. Just freezing federal tax expenditures would reduce the deficit by over $50 billion.

Question 3: Won't a tax increase or increased revenues cause a recession, as the President insists?

No. There is no general rule on that question; a recession depends on many economic variables. In fact, in 1981 there was a tax cut but a recession followed a tax cut. In 1982 federal taxes rose, but we have had a steady building of the economy since then.

Question 4: What really has happened to federal aid in the last five years or so?

Federal aid to cities has been cut from $69 billion in 1980 to about $17 billion proposed this last year. Gramm-Rudman and the new budget will likely result in the elimination of the federal partnership with cities and towns over its five-year life. Having rigged the game the way I described, the only outcome can be elimination of all federal programs over time.

Question 5: What will happen to and in cities if Gramm-Rudman operates for five years without a major federal tax increase?

If Gramm-Rudman continues for five years, all federal aid to local governments will likely be eliminated. But because such a small portion of the federal deficit is subject to Gramm-Rudman (only 13 percent), the federal deficit itself will remain after the dismantlement of the working relationship that has been so arduously and carefully built up over all these years.

Question 6: How do you reconcile your call for closing tax expenditures and your vigorous lobbying to retain the deductibility of state and local taxes and the tax exemption for interest on bonds?

Tax expenditures are incentives built into the federal tax code to encourage certain types of activities, but the deductibility of state and local taxes and the tax-exempt bonds were not put into the code to encourage constituents to pay property taxes. They were already paying property taxes. It was a constitutional recognition of a partnership, of a relationship; not an incentive device as all of the other provisions in the code, but a recognition of another level of government.

Question 7: Federal aid is down, local taxes may go up. You call that passing the buck, but isn't that really the best way to finance these activities so they address local need?

No. Federal spending of money coming from our cities and towns is up, but aid back to our municipalities is down. There is a question of priorities. Why should we be spending more in foreign aid and eliminating domestic aid? Second, not all cities and towns have the same capacity to raise their own local taxes. Some cities and towns have to provide a disproportionate level of services, because they have a very poor community and also a poor tax base. So the structure of the tradeoff is just not fair. We will force, for example, people to rely less on a progressive income tax and more on regressive local fees.

Question 8: More than a majority of cities seem to be doing all right. Why then are you so insistent about the dire effects of Gramm-Rudman and the loss of federal aid? Aren't you exaggerating and painting an unnecessarily bleak picture just in order to rationalize keeping federal aid programs for your constituency?

The cities have sacrificed, have cut, and have raised taxes, year after year. Some cities are in good shape, but many (especially in regions beset by economic turndowns) are at the end of their ropes. Poverty is up in America, unemployment is up in America, and tax caps have been thrown in place. Cities truthfully, honestly have a more difficult time; and I think that point needs to be gotten across.

Question 9: How can you support General Revenue Sharing, when there is no revenue to share—especially when General Revenue Sharing goes to so many wealthy jurisdictions?

General Revenue Sharing was not created to share methodical federal revenues or surpluses. It was created to help comply with federal mandates, but it is shared according to need. The lower the average income of your city's taxpayers, the greater the revenue sharing amount. When President Nixon signed Revenue Sharing into law there was a federal deficit then. Since 1972, when revenue sharing was enacted, federal funding for revenue sharing has been cut, but the deficit has grown by 1,000 percent.

Question 10: Finally, are the governors right when they say that the federal role should be basically national defense and Medicaid, but all other programs such as housing, environment, education and transportation should be left to the states?

The answer, we feel, is no. Providing a decent, safe and sanitary house for all Americans has been a federal goal since 1937. Cleaning the nation's air and water is a national problem; we can't have 50 different sets of laws and standards for bodies of air and water that don't respect state borders because of their natural layout. Giving our children a quality education must be a national priority for the future of our country. Providing the American people access to schools and jobs and health care on the waters, highways, rails, and airs is fundamental to a national economy. So the states have an important role to play but so does the federal government. The proof of the need for federal aid is the costly mandates in each and every area imposed upon us.

In other words, the federal government cares enough about these questions to set down regulations and laws thereby defining its interest in the subject—defining a role for the federal government, but it's withdrawing from the financing of those activities.

As I said to you this morning, I think we have a tremendous opportunity.

I came away from Seattle [the 1985 Congress of Cities] totally depressed, beset by a feeling of gloom. I didn't see a sliver of daylight in an otherwise solid wall of obstruction and opposition. But it seems to me that as we get closer to the day of reckoning on these questions there is some reason for some measure of, if not open optimism, then at least a hard sense of determination.

First of all, I think we are going to get some movement on that re-enactment date on the bonds, on that effective date of the bonds as you heard Mr. Rostenkowski suggest this morning, but we have to work on that.

I think we will see some movement on state and local tax deductibility, but you have to work on that.

I think we'll see some movement on the tax-exempt bond question, but you can determine whether that actually happens. And on the question of the programs, I think that as the congressmen realize what is actually going to happen, you are going to see some opening of daylight for compromise.

But it's got to be in a spirit of clear determination on our part. There is not one moment that can be wasted, not one iota of energy wasted on apologizing for the cities' role in this country or for their place in this system.

We have a place to roam, to play; it is an honorable one, and I cannot tell you in words just how important. Because what I think is at stake here is a lot more than just the cities, as important as they are. I think what is at stake here is a lot more than some federal titles in a law, as important as that is. I think what is at stake is a lot more than some budgetary appropriations.

What's at stake here is an American way of life, in which we have set some ideals. This country works so that all its people have a measure of justice and opportunity, prosperity, and, yes, equality.

We teach little children at five years of age their first day in school to recite words that they don't even understand at that point, and that's the Pledge of Allegiance. We teach them as they say that to close with the phrase, "one nation under God, indivisible, with liberty and justice for all."

One nation, not the Sunbelt against the Frostbelt, not the big cities against the little cities, not the defense industry pitted against the needs of the homeless or day care.

One nation under God—a God who can see just as easily into the homes of those senior citizens, who wait in the cold scared about whether or not the programs that they depend on are going to continue—just as easily as he can see into the skybox suites of the modern stadiums.

Indivisible, not divided, white against black, rich against poor, with liberty and justice for all. And if we lose that sense, we lose something else in this country—a country that fundamentally believes in a sense of equality, so that people are willing to work their hearts out now knowing that there's something better out there for them and their children.

If we lose that quality of people sacrificing now for the future, then we will end up no more than a nation in a constant adversarial hostility, as people have to demand right this minute everything because there is no faith in the future.

Ladies and gentlemen, the stakes here are a lot bigger than our individual cities, or even laws, or even grant programs. The stakes are a vision of our country, and the cities have had and will continue to have a place in that system. A lot of how it comes out is up to you and what you do over the course of the next 24 hours.

LET US FINISH THE TASK[1]

VERNON E. JORDAN, JR.[2]

In an address that he called "a bit of a homecoming," Vernon E. Jordan, Jr., spoke to 300 members of the Lawyers Club of Atlanta on March 19, 1986. Making a speech to that particular group might also be described as a Horatio Alger story, a testimonial to democratic government, and a declaration of faith in the people of the United States. Jordan, one of the most eloquent and influential black leaders in the country, was invited to address a club that, in his youth, was one of the city's most elitist organizations and strongest defenders of segregation. As a teenager and young man, he had listened avidly to the lawyers' speeches while helping his mother cater club dinners. He returned to the club more than 30 years later, not as a waiter or menial, but as a distinguished national leader, with his mother and other family members present as honored guests.

As president of the National Urban League from 1972-1981, Jordan closely monitored the progress of civil rights legislation and the condition of blacks in this country. Since stepping down as leader of that organization, he has continued to address problems and issues affecting not only black, but also white, Americans.

In his speech to the Atlanta lawyers, Jordan noted that as change has come to the Lawyers' Club, so it "has come to the entire South and the nation." The occasion afforded Jordan the opportunity not only to review the history of the civil rights movement and black gains, but also to remind his listeners of what remains to be accomplished. Asserting that complacency is the greatest danger and that "we have a long way to go," Jordan commented, noting that

> black disadvantage is national in scope and represents the nation's major domestic problem. Widespread poverty and unemployment damage our economy, prevent full use of our productive resources at a time of global economic competition, and threaten a democracy that is based on full consent of the governed.

Jordan went on to discuss the political ramifications of black disadvantage. In strong terms, he accused the Reagan administration of a lack of concern for the welfare of the blacks and predicted that "Republicans will not hold on to the White House in the post-Reagan era unless they can cut across class lines and make inroads in the black vote." Democrats too "will have to broaden their base if they hope to return to national dominance." Jordan anticipated the emergence of the South as a leading force in national politics and urged that his listeners "as southerners and

[1]Delivered to the Lawyers Club of Atlanta at its regular monthly dinner meeting in a banquet room in the Omni International Hotel at 7:30 P.M., March 19, 1986.

[2]For a biographical note, see Appendix.

as lawyers well and truly finish the task of making ours an open, pluralistic, integrated society that all Americans may be proud of."

Vernon E. Jordan, Jr.'s speech: I cannot come before you, at this place and at this time, without thinking of a thirteen-year-old youngster who participated in his first Lawyers' Club dinner many years ago. He came earlier than the guests, by way of the freight elevator rather than the main one.

None of the guests noticed him, for they did not see him, or if they did, they paid him no mind. While they were putting the final touches on legal briefs and hurrying to Fairlie Street, he was setting up tables, and the bar, and doing all the things that have to be done to make a function like this one possible.

His mother catered the dinner. She prepared those filet mignons that the youngster brought into the building and that the dinner guests enjoyed so much. After the tables were cleared, the speeches started. That youngster was supposed to be in the kitchen, helping to clean up. But he was an inquisitive kid, and he would sneak off, unseen, to listen to the speeches.

To say he was impressed would be an understatement. He was awed by the dignity of the occasion, by the brilliance of the oratory, by the image of wealth and power given off by the guests. His experience led him to dream of being a lawyer, of talking like those speakers, of dressing like those distinguished guests.

That first dinner he attended was back in 1948, and from that year until 1953 he never missed a Lawyers' Club dinner. At each one, the same story was repeated: setting up the tables and the bar, helping to clean up after dinner, and sneaking off to listen to the worldly men talk about the law and the issues of the day.

Then he went off to college and to law school. But whenever his visits home coincided with a dinner, he would come to help out, wait on tables, and sneak back to listen to the speeches. He heard a lot and saw a lot in those days, and when he returned home with a law degree in his pocket and a $35-a-week job in Don Hollowell's law office that specialized in civil rights, he knew that he would not become a member of the Lawyers' Club.

That was only in part because he was black, and the Lawyers' Club, like other Atlanta institutions, was segregated. But it was also because the club was one of the most elitist of Atlanta's elite institutions. Many times that young man saw the box being passed, and many times he saw white lawyers denied membership.

Some of the older members here tonight may remember the fine meals they enjoyed between 1948 and 1960, when they were catered by my mother, Mary Jordan. She is here tonight, not as a vendor, but as a guest. And while I am a bit older and, I hope, wiser, I am still very much the same young man who helped make those dinners come off and who hid in the back to listen to speeches.

Tonight I am here to make a speech myself. I must say the view from the podium is better than the view from the kitchen. As you can tell from my story, I consider this evening a signal honor, and a bit of a homecoming.

I suppose that my being here is an example of how much the Lawyers' Club has changed. But not only has change come to this venerable institution, it has come to the entire South and the nation.

Remember that the South once clung to segregation with a fervor hard to imagine these days. The cry was: "No, not one!", and George Wallace barred the schoolhouse door.

Today the South is the least segregated part of the country east of the Rockies, and George Wallace is elected with the help of black people, whom he once tried to keep from exercising their right to vote. The South has changed, and by changing, it can light a beacon for the rest of the nation. It has experienced the worst of racism and today is experiencing the promise of integration.

But perhaps the greatest danger our region faces is the danger of complacency, the idea that because we've come so far so soon, we have reached our goal. But if the goal is a truly multiracial South in which each and every one of us can develop his or her potential to the fullest, we have a long way to go.

I believe southerners should be asking themselves whether the South has changed enough, and whether that change is in the process of being arrested as part of the national withdrawal from efforts to make our society more equal and more just. The challenge today is to make the South the engine of racial progress that helps bring the rest of the country into the twenty-first century.

The South has changed politically. The Voting Rights Act of 1965 and the civil rights law made it possible for the two-party system to come to the region, for a southerner to be elected President of the United States, and for the South to participate in the mainstream of the national economy.

But in racial terms, the South has not changed enough in the economic sphere. The challenge of our times, for the region and for the nation, is to achieve the economic empowerment of black Americans. Unless the racial gap is closed in the economic sphere, there is a danger that the racial politics of the past will continue far into the future, with racially based class divisions becoming the determining factor in the region's socio-political makeup.

That danger is national, as well. For black disadvantage is national in scope, and represents the nation's major domestic problem. Widespread poverty and unemployment damage our economy, prevent full use of our productive resources at a time of global economic competition, and threaten a democracy that is based on the full consent and participation of the governed.

Unfortunately, there is a growing feeling, spurred by the Reagan Administration, that race is no longer a significant factor in American life. The Attorney General has campaigned long and hard for the view that we are a color-blind, racially neutral society. His Justice Department has expended time and energy better used to enforce the civil rights laws, papering the federal courts with briefs arguing against affirmative action and other civil rights measures. The administration has spent months in internal debate over issuing an executive order that would revoke present orders mandating affirmative action for federal contractors. And the Equal Employment Opportunity Commission has changed its guidelines relating to hiring goals and timetables.

The Supreme Court has considered several affirmative action cases and has several more on this session's calendar. Its decision in the *Stotts* case, in 1984, affirming the precedence of seniority agreements over affirmative action in layoffs, triggered a wave of misinterpretations by federal lawyers. The Justice Department's attempt to broaden the ruling far beyond the obvious limits of the case has given new heart to those who would dismantle affirmative action programs.

One of the cases before the Court, involving New York City's sheetmetal union, seeks to overturn a federal court order requiring the union to comply with an affirmative action plan. The Justice Department, which is supporting the union, admits that the union has "an ample record of inexcusable disobedience." But it would allow that disobedience to stand.

That typifies the administration's approach. It agrees that blacks were persistently denied their civil rights, that constitutional rights were violated, and that race was the grounds for exclusion. But at the same time it resists racially based remedies that the courts have consistently ruled were constitutional and that offer the only means of reversing admittedly unconstitutional practices.

It should listen to Justice Blackmun, who wrote in the *Bakke* case:

> In order to get beyond racism we must first take account of race. There is no other way. And in order to treat some persons equally, we must treat them differently.

That seems to me to be self-evident. We cannot erase the burden of past and present discrimination without a temporary period of affirmative action to open opportunities for those denied them for so long.

Even as the administration attempts to stigmatize affirmative action with the label of "reverse discrimination," affirmative action enjoys the support of the business community. Business sees affirmative action as a common sense way to solve the problem of underrepresentation of minorities and women. As the National Association of Manufacturers told a congressional committee last summer:

> Industry does not believe that numerical goals for minority inclusion in the workforce, by themselves, constitute quotas. Business, particularly big business, sets goals and timetables for every aspect of its operation. . . . Setting goals and timetables for minority and female participation is a way of measuring progress and focusing on potential discrimination.

At a time when black gains are eroding and the gap between the races is widening dangerously, affirmative action is more important than ever before. We are *not* a color-blind society. We are *not* a racially neutral society. We are still a society in which race counts; a society in which blackness is a badge of inequality. Lyndon Johnson said it well:

> To be black in a white society is not to stand on level and equal ground. While the races may stand side by side, whites stand on history's mountain and blacks stand in history's hollow. Until we overcome unequal history, we cannot overcome unequal opportunity.

The South knows a lot about overcoming unequal history. As a region, it has been the poor sister of the rest of the nation. Politically, it has been relegated to the margins of the national polity.

Thanks to the destruction of Jim Crow, to the civil rights laws, and to the achievement of a more democratic political life in the region, the South now has a greater influence in the political life of the nation.

I cannot stress too strongly that without the inclusion of black citizens, the South would have forever remained cut off from the mainstream of American politics. But the civil rights revolution that brought the South's black citizens full participation in voting revolutionized southern politics and helped make the region a positive factor in national politics.

It was the black vote that made Jimmy Carter president in 1976, and that brought progressive leaders to the state houses and to Congress. It was the elimination of racism as a political strategy that enables the South to stand tall because it is represented by people like Sam Nunn, Dick Riley, Bill Clinton, and Chuck Robb, instead of hanging its head in shame because it was represented by the Talmadges, Bilbos, and Eastlands of another era.

To be sure, the Congressional delegation includes the likes of Jesse Helms and Strom Thurmond, but their day is fading, their language has moderated, and they no longer typify the main thrust of southern politics. The new legitimacy of southern politics suggests that the region will play a key role in deciding the 1988 election.

The so-called realignment of national politics has not taken place. Republican dominance is confined to the White House. Republican control of the Senate is shaky, and the Democrats are firmly in control of the House and of state governments. The President's political dominance has been a personal triumph that has failed to extend to either his party or his philosophy. Even as they voted for Ronald Reagan twice, Americans, as measured by polls and by their other political behavior, reject his anti-government, anti-social programs positions.

In 1988 the big question will be: Is there life after Reagan? And it's a question for both parties.

The answer for the Republicans will be a resounding "no" if they continue to reject black aspirations and insult black voters. New Jersey's Governor Kean recently said that the Republicans can become the majority party "if we reach out to all classes, all races, all sectors of society." He is right.

American politics today are dangerously close to being a regional politics, with the Democrats strong in the Northeast and the industrial Midwest and the Republicans representing the West and the white South.

Our politics are also more blatantly class-based than in the past. President Reagan's 1984 sweep can be compared to Eisenhower's 1956 victory. Both got 75 percent of the vote of the richest ten percent. But the resemblance ends there. Ike won 56 percent of the working and lower middle class vote—Reagan only 43 percent. Ike even won the vote of the poorest ten percent, getting 59 percent of their ballots. Reagan got less than a third.

Republicans will not hold on to the White House in the post-Reagan era unless they can cut across class lines and make inroads in the black vote. Without the President's personality to attract voters otherwise opposed to his policies, the party will have to broaden its base. And it must do so on issues, not on personality, because the post-Reagan Republicans don't have anyone with the President's charm and mass appeal.

The Democrats, too, will have to broaden their base if they hope to return to national dominance. Above all, that means reaching out to the South by placing a southerner on the national ticket in 1988.

The Democrats have a wealth of candidates for 1988, and a southern talent pool as rich as it has ever been. The emergence of southern political leaders who can appeal to a national constituency is a major strength of the party. But they can't treat that talent pool the way Republicans have treated blacks—by ignoring it. A southerner on the national ticket can bring the Southern white vote back home while holding on to the increasingly important black vote.

The Democrats can't win without the black vote. And they can't win without the South. The two are not mutually exclusive. If anything, they complement each other. The stage is set for the reconstruction of a national coalition that includes professionals, workers, blacks, and the South.

The Democrats have the potential to construct a viable coalition that is far broader-based than the narrow Republican coalition that has been in power. Whether they have the wisdom to do it is another question.

I am hopeful they will because it holds the potential of bringing more rational policies to the national scene, and because it can be the seal on the South's emergence to national leadership and political maturity. Above all, the inclusion of southern leadership in a national coalition devoted to restoring the values of justice and fairness in our national life will help the South and the nation complete the job it started some two decades ago.

I have talked tonight about the gap between our aspirations and our achievements, about the need to achieve black economic empowerment, about the need to implement affirmative action programs that help us to meet that goal. And I have talked about the South's re-entry into the nation's political life, and removing the burden of race from our region's and our nation's life.

As we consider the sweep of time and look to the future, we can better understand that only by constructing an open, pluralistic, integrated society can America survive into the twenty-first century. Only by overcoming the inequalities that still permeate our society can we build a nation whose decency matches its prosperity, and whose unity propels it to new, higher levels of accomplishment.

And in the struggle to reach for the heights of a better society, each and every one of us must play a constructive role. Each of us must reach out to others; each of us must overcome the artificial barriers of class and race to assert our humanity and our solidarity with other citizens of our national family.

We began that great adventure in the civil rights era of the 1960s. And now it is our task—and especially the task of the legal profession that wields so much power in America—to complete that great adventure of the American spirit.

Four hundred years ago, the great English adventurer Sir Francis Drake wrote, "It isn't the beginning of the task, but the continuing of the same until it be well and truly finished wherein lies the true glory."

Let us then, as southerners and as lawyers, well and truly finish the task of making ours an open, pluralistic, integrated society that all Americans may be proud of.

PRESIDENTIAL PRIMARIES[1]

CHARLES T. MANATT[2]

Concerned with the length and cost of the presidential primary system, former President Gerald R. Ford organized the Conference on Presidential Primaries, which was held on April 24-26, 1985, at the Ford Presidential Library at the University of Michigan in Ann Arbor. The purpose of the meeting, according to the conference program, was "to develop recommendations for improving the way in which presidential candidates are presented to the voters and chosen for party nomination." The conference brought together some 30 experts—political candidates, campaign advisors, press secretaries, scholars, and research foundation representatives—who debated and discussed the topics of campaign spending, media coverage, the role of the parties, and the best means of changing the system. The conference met in six sessions and included formal papers, commentary by panels of respondents, and a final wrap-up discussion and charge to the participants.

While the two days of lively discussion and deliberation produced some recommendations, few solutions emerged. One of the participants and director of the Ford Library, Don Wilson, commented, "This group knows too much to give sharp, decisive prescriptions. . . . We did not intend that this conference would solicit answers, not at this stage. The purpose of the conference was to identify and illuminate the problems and stimulate public awareness about the presidential nominating system. President Ford believes the conference achieved these goals" (*Gerald R. Ford Foundation Newsletter*, Spring, 1985, p. 1).

Among the many distinguished speakers at the conference was Charles T. Manatt, the former chairman of the Democratic Party, who spoke on the subject of presidential primaries. Manatt was the keynote speaker at a conference banquet attended by 350 people. His address was preceded by introductions by the President of the University of Michigan, musical entertainment by the Friars Ensemble of the Men's Glee Club of the university, and remarks by Marvin Esch of the American Enterprise Institute.

In his speech, Manatt praised former President Ford, saying that he "left our land better than he found it." He then pointed out that "Gerald Ford's service did not end with his presidency. It continues today, at this library, with this conference and with others like it. We are here not only to reflect on the past, but to set a direction for the future of one of the most vital questions of our political system: the way in which we choose our presidents." Urging a bipartisan approach to reduce the spiralling cost and increasing length of presidential campaigns, Manatt noted that this was a particularly appropriate time to act because it presented a nearly unique opportunity for change:

[1]Delivered to the Conference on Presidential Primaries as the keynote address at a banquet held at the Michigan League, the University of Michigan, Ann Arbor, Michigan, at 9:00 P.M. on April 25, 1985.

[2]For biographical note, see Appendix.

> For the first time in 28 years, in 1988 neither party will have an incumbent president eligible for re-election. Together both parties can shape and seek changes on the basis of merit, and not the calculus of individual interest. They can move in Congress . . . to mandate steps toward goals which virtually everyone professes, but no one so far seems able to achieve.

After outlining a plan for revising the presidential primary system, Manatt urged that Americans meet the challenge with, in Gerald Ford's words, "instincts of openness and candor."

Charles T. Manatt's speech: I am honored to be here, first, because the subject is important. Second, because the company is distinguished, and, most of all, because I have a special respect for President Gerald Ford and I share the abiding affection of the American people for him and for the great service he performed for our country.

More than a decade has passed since the solemn and difficult day when he took the oath of office and promised to restore the trust and confidence of this nation. He kept his oath and he kept his promise. There were Democrats, including me, who disagreed with some of his policies and, as President Ford knows, we said so clearly and vigorously. But we can all agree on something else, much more important, which cannot be said so clearly and unequivocally of every presidency: Gerald Ford left our land better than he found it. His decency truly did make us proud to be Americans; his tenure truly did make it possible to move beyond some of the darkest times of our national life. And for that, Mr. President, you have the gratitude of your fellow citizens and you will always have a high place in our history.

Gerald Ford's service did not end with his presidency. It continues today, at this library, with this conference and with others like it. We are here not only to reflect on the past, but to set a direction for the future on one of the most vital questions of our political system: the way in which we choose our presidents.

Except for prescribing the time of the election and the function of the electoral college, the Constitution is remarkably silent on this question. There is not a single word about political parties or nominating methods and there was no provision even for the separate election of the president and the vice-president, until Aaron Burr nearly tricked Thomas Jefferson out of his victory of 1800.

The framers had George Washington consciously in mind as their first President, and they seem almost unconsciously to have treated him as the model for all future elections—someone who could emerge as a consensus choice, on the basis of past service and not partisan appeals.

Events swiftly confounded any such expectation. Madison and Hamilton, who had decried factions in *The Federalist Papers*, soon joined others in founding opposing political parties. Each sought the presidency in different years; one of them succeeded and the other failed.

Since then, for nearly two centuries, we have invented, amended, blamed, and praised the means of picking presidential nominees. We have moved from King Caucus to what we regard as an open process, where voters are supposed to have a direct and decisive say. The present period of change began, in a sense, in 1936, when Franklin Roosevelt in effect commanded the Democratic convention to repeal the two-thirds rule which had nearly denied him the nomination four years before. The immediate effect was to deprive the southern states of their traditional veto power. The longer-range result was to foster the idea that convention rules—once thought to be a sacrosanct part of an implicit yet delicately balanced compact, or an inviolate matter of states' rights—could be reformulated or "reformed" at will, at the national level.

But after the 1936 convention, nothing else of great consequence changed in the rules for more than three decades. I suspect the reason was the tendency of the parties to nominate the most popular candidates. When, arguably, they failed to do so—for example, in the Stevenson-Kefauver contest of 1952—the contestants represented no fundamental cleavage of issues or ideology within the party and the supporters of the loser soon rallied to the winner. That same year, perhaps such a cleavage did exist among Republicans, but who could persuasively contend that Dwight Eisenhower was not the choice of the people and, therefore, he was and had to be the nominee of a rigged or unfair convention?

Yet there were also pressures, related more to the emerging civil rights movement than to the identity of any particular nominee, which were building beneath the surface and which would augment the coming wave of reform. Democratic conventions hotly debated whether to require "loyalty oaths"—pledges in advance to support the national ticket—as a condition of seating delegates. In 1964, the Mississippi Freedom Democratic Party challenged the regular Mississippi delegation—and the resulting compromise settlement, negotiated by the young Attorney General of Minnesota, Walter Mondale, put the national party squarely into the business of regulating delegate selection in the state of Mississippi.

The precedents and pressures were there and the 1968 convention provided the spark that set off a chain reaction of reform which has not yet spent itself. In 1968, there was an impression, right or wrong—and this is not the place to decide—that the eventual nominee, Hubert Humphrey, who had not entered a single primary, was not the popular choice. And the critics could point to some glaring examples of apparent unfairness: a Georgia delegation picked personally by the governor with no democratic participation or recourse; a Texas delegation with the unit rule, forcing the opponents of the Vietnam War within that delegation to cast a vote in favor of it; other delegations, selected far in advance of the convention, long before the campaigns of Robert Kennedy and Eugene McCarthy, and even longer before the withdrawal of Lyndon Johnson.

Added to this was the rising call for the empowerment of new forces, with blacks now joined by Hispanics, the young, and women, who were starting to express a new and powerful consciousness of their own identity. To conciliate these forces, and as part of the effort to rescue his candidacy from the chaos of the Chicago convention, Hubert Humphrey agreed to establish a commission to rewrite the rules for 1972 and beyond.

This history points to an important insight: The reforms were not an accident, but a result of irrepressible events and broader trends. It also suggests that while the rules can be, and have been, amended repeatedly, the reforms, in their fundamental aspects, cannot be rolled back. The Republican party, which was not the crucible of these changes, has adopted many of them. One reason is that state laws which apply to both parties were adopted to accommodate the new Democratic reforms. But the other reason, more pervasive and powerful, is that the rules changes reflected real changes in American society, changes which either party could ignore only at its peril. At the 1984 Dallas convention, Republicans denounced quotas and then celebrated the fact that nearly half of their delegates were women.

There are two presently fashionable reactions of this period of reform both of which I reject.

I do not accept the notion that the old system produced better nominees and that somehow it did so precisely because of its rules. Any such argument depends on selective history and on the assumption that the nominating process can be made into a special preserve, sealed off from the mood and movements of the times. The old system produced Harding and Nixon as well as Eisenhower and Kennedy. And the Democrats had fewer chances to make mistakes in those years, not because the rules protected us, but because the unprecedented four terms of Franklin Roosevelt prevented us for a long time from nominating someone else. On the other hand, who imagines that the old rules could have survived the transformation of modern communications and consciousness? After Watergate, could the Republicans or the Democrats really have chosen their nominee in a smoke-filled room? And if the choice in 1984 had been left to party leaders and not primaries, would it have been any different given that so many of those leaders had already decided to endorse Walter Mondale by the end of 1983?

Just as I reject the notion that the old was better, so I also reject the fashionable argument that what we have now is good enough and that it cannot or should not be improved. On our side, revisions in the rules will not cure all that ails the Democratic party or, on the other side, alter the underlying factors which could undermine the present Republican success. But revisions can make the system more rational, less beholden to separate groups, and more reflective of the national will.

This is not only an appropriate time to act; it also presents nearly a unique opportunity for change. For the first time in 28 years, in 1988 neither party will have an incumbent president eligible for re-election. Together both parties can shape and seek changes on the basis of merit, and not the calculus of individual interest. They can move in Congress, in ways which I will outline, to mandate steps toward goals which virtually everyone professes, but no one so far seems able to achieve.

The critical cause of that shortfall is that we have considered the question largely in the context of party commissions, which themselves have largely been dominated by the representatives and adherents of prospective candidates. Congress offers a different forum which can focus on broader purposes and which can invoke effective powers of enforcement.

First, Congressional action is not only the best way to deal with the length of the process, it may be the only way. Federal legislation can deny matching funds to candidates who violate federal guidelines.

Those guidelines should set primaries on four dates: the first or second Tuesdays in March, April, May, and June. Caucuses could be held anytime in the week following the primaries. To avoid the distortion of having all the states in a single region vote on the same day, without the balancing impact of a more representative diversity, Congress should consider the concept of time zone primaries. And which time zone went first and which followed in any given year should be determined by lottery. For the 1988 campaign, the lottery should be held in December 1986.

Any candidate who participated in a nonapproved delegate selection process, held outside the system, would lose federal matching funds.

As a former national chairman, I saw what happened when we tried, on our own, to shorten the process for 1984. We made some progress: Iowa came five weeks later than in 1980 and New Hampshire a week later; but it proved virtually impossible to do more, especially to eliminate the special status of the two states. There is always at least one candidate who will parade as their defender and the others can't afford to be seen as the ones who tried to deny Iowa or New Hampshire their rightful priority. So those states can pick their dates, regardless of party rules, and assume that by the time the convention comes, the winning candidate won't let it refuse to seat their delegates. And imagine the plight of the candidates who had to campaign in the New Hampshire primary after trying to abolish it. The issue wouldn't be the economy, or Central America, new ideas or old values, but why did they try to deprive the state of its place in the news and its lion's share of campaign revenues.

This is no way to pick a president. In 1984, candidates had to pay, according to price list, to put up banners or posters at a New Hampshire party event. They even had to pay a price to speak. Perhaps there's a rough justice in that, at least when it comes to some political speakers we've all heard; but practices like this degrade not only the candidates, but the process. They don't advance the cause of picking a nominee; they exploit it.

New Hampshire makes no more sense as the first primary for selecting a Democratic nominee than Massachusetts would as the first primary for the Republicans. And although I was raised in Iowa, and I'll certainly hear about this when I go back, Iowa has no special claim and it deserves no automatic priority.

The system I suggest also has the advantage of inviting a more coherent and less debilitating dialogue. In 1983 and 1984, we saw an increasing proliferation of joint appearances, debates, and speech contests, often used by state parties as fund-raising vehicles. Too readily, these events tempt candidates, especially those who are behind, to launch the kind of attacks which can almost fatally weaken a likely nominee for the coming campaign. What we need is a greater certainty of debates in the general election and greater control over the number and intensity of the exchanges during the primary period. Perhaps as part of the reform I've proposed, the national parties should each sponsor four debates in 1988 on the four Saturdays or Sundays before the designated primary dates.

But any plan to shorten the length of the process will be only half successful if it fails to deal with the straw polls which foster an early start and a relentlessly paced campaign. Here, again, I believe that the matching funds system provides a mechanism for reform. The law should be amended so that any contributions raised before October 1st in the year preceding the primaries won't be eligible for a federal match. Candidates could raise enough to sustain a pre-primary operation; but they would be unlikely to raise more and more in unmatchable money to compete in unsanctioned straw polls.

To me, October 1st certainly is a reasonable date to start the match. A quarter of a century ago, John Kennedy was counted as an early entry because he announced his candidacy on January 3rd, 1960. And the crucial organizing meeting of his campaign was held in October of 1959. Perhaps we can't restore that sense of proportion to the process; but at least we can moderate a situation in which we are perilously close to the moment, in Adlai Stevenson's words, when the nominee will be "the last survivor." The precondition of running for president should not be that a candidate is out of office or that he or she has to neglect totally, for two or three years, the office they may already hold.

The other major problem, the other perennial complaint about the system, is its cost. Frankly, I don't believe that we're going to find a way to nominate presidents on the cheap. But we can develop a way to reduce the dominance of fund-raising in campaigns. One step is something I've already discussed, to limit matching for 1988 to contributions given after October 1st, 1987. At the same time, we should raise the limit on an individual contribution to $2,000 and we should match the first thousand dollars, rather than just the first $250.

There is no reason to hold candidates hostage to limits set a decade ago and which, in real dollars, are worth only half as much today.

And there is no reason to make it progressively harder to raise money, to make candidates allocate more and more of their time searching out more contributors, simply so they will have barely resources enough to compete in the first primaries.

Yet wouldn't an October 1st date for matching work to precisely the opposite effect, forcing candidates to put greater energy into fund-raising later in the process? But they could gather pledges in advance; they could draw up budgets. All this rule says is that they could not actually receive or spend contributions before October 1st, if they wanted to see that money matched.

In closing, let me reaffirm my belief that in the truest sense, we can only reform the primary process if we reach beyond traditional candidate rivalries and across the usual partisan divisions. Republicans and Democrats in Congress can bring about changes that separately the Republican and Democratic national committees probably can never achieve.

And there is no better place to begin, to reflect on where we have been, and to define where we should go, than here at this library, which honors President Ford. He was a partisan, a strong and committed one. But as president, he also reminded us, in word and deed, that our opponents were not our enemies. In his inaugural address, Thomas Jefferson told a divided country, "We are all Federalists; we are all Republicans." In his years in office, Gerald Ford taught a wounded, disillusioned nation that, in the end, we are all Democrats and we are all Republicans—because we are all Americans.

In that spirit, let us meet the challenges before us whether they involve the way we nominate presidents, or the way we conduct our national debates on the great issues. Let us work with each other where we can, disagree when we must, and set a high standard of civility and mutual respect. In short, let us remember the plain majesty of Gerry Ford's own inaugural message that no matter how vigorous the debate between us, it is really "just a little straight talk among friends," that the bond between us, "though strained, is unbroken," and that most of all, it depends on "instincts of openness and candor."

A DIFFERENT PERSPECTIVE

WE'VE JUST BEGUN[1]

ELEANOR C. SMEAL[2]

In July, 1985, Eleanor Smeal, who headed the National Organization of Women (NOW) from 1977 to 1982, was again elected president of the feminist group. She made her first major speech after taking office to the National Press Club in Washington, D.C., on September 5, 1985. The National Press Club hosts from 70 to 90 speeches each year and is one of the capital's, and, indirectly, the nation's, best forums for the discussion of public issues. Smeal's speech was part of the club's regular luncheon series.

In her address, Smeal reiterated the central theme of her campaign for the NOW presidency. The main issue in the NOW election was the degree and kind of activism that the organization should adopt. During a contest characterized by some bitterness, she accused the incumbent, Judy Goldsmith, of inadequate leadership and vigor. Contending that the New Right has long been an enemy of the women's movement, Smeal urges feminists to take a more aggressive role in opposing the rising tide of conservatism. In her speech to the press club, she maintained that it was time "to raise hell, to spread the word, to organize women. Because there is no question in my mind but that rights are never won unless people are willing to fight for them."

Following her reelection as NOW president, Smeal embarked on a schedule of giving up to a dozen speeches a week, sometimes delivering as many as three a day. She has addressed unions, college students, and feminist groups, including NOW chapters. In her speeches she has likened the New Right to the Nazis, saying they oppose personal freedoms, such as birth control and abortion, and attack the patriotism of anyone who disagrees with them. "'They say we're anti-family, anti-God. They are all code words for calling us communists. For too long, we decided not to respond to their charges. Well, I have decided to deal with it.' In her speeches, Smeal doesn't name names, unless asked to do so. And then she offers a list, including the Reverend Jerry Falwell and [Phyllis] Shafly, various conservative groups, and a host of anti-abortion organizations" (Thomas Ferraro, Baton Rouge *Advocate*, December 29, 1985, p. 7C).

Smeal has a reputation as an effective debater and public speaker, which she attributes largely to growing up in an Italian family. A Phi Beta graduate of Duke University, the wife of a business consultant, and a mother of two, she is a former homemaker turned activist. Ann Lewis, a longtime NOW member and national director of Americans for Demo-

[1]Address to the National Press Club, Washington, D.C., presented at 1:00 P.M., December 5, 1985, in the club ballroom.

[2]For biographical note, see Appendix.

cratic Action, has noted, "'She is a superb technician and one of the very few charismatic leaders of either gender I know in the United States today'" (Thomas Ferraro, Baton Rouge *Advocate*, December 29, 1985, p. 7C). Of Smeal's lashing out at the New Right and calling them "fascists," Lewis observed, "'I can't think of another woman leader who would do it. It's not their style'" (Thomas Ferraro, Baton Rouge *Advocate*, December 29, 1985, p. 7C).

Smeal delivered the National Press Club speech to an audience of approximately 300 NOW supporters, club members, and reporters. The *New York Times* reported that her voice rose with the volume of applause during her speech, which was followed by a question and answer period (Phil Gailey, September 6, 1985, p. 7).

Eleanor C. Smeal's speech: If I ever doubted whether it was time to raise hell, all I had to do was read today's newspapers. The three-judge panel of the Ninth Circuit Court said that the 1964 Civil Rights Act does not obligate the state of Washington to eliminate an economic inequality which it did not create. That's the great principle in jurisprudence of Adam and Eve. Take it to your creator. God knows that man, who created this system of injustice that we work under, has no responsibility.

A lot of people would ask me what my reaction to that decision is. I say it's only fighting mad. We intend to break out of the ghetto of low wages that has been created for us one way or another.

What the Washington case shows is that we have to fight simultaneously on several fronts. While we were fighting in the court, we were also fighting in the state legislature in Washington state. The Washington state legislature has passed a law there that says by 1993 they are going to have pay equity in the state system and, in fact, the legislature has passed a $42 million back pay appropriation to help correct the inequity. There would have been no gains there if we had not fought the court case.

I believe the Washington state case set off a revolution in the fight to break out of the wage ghetto for women. And right now, throughout this country, in some 100 jurisdictions, similar pay equity cases are being fought through the courts. Or we're pursuing legislation at the state level. Or we're pursuing county commission ordinances to change the inequities.

And, as we fight in these arenas, where the real battle is taking place is in the court of public opinion. This three-man panel in the Ninth Circuit did not make this decision in a vacuum. They read the newspapers. They read what the right wing is saying, what business is saying. They know only too well what the opposition is saying about comparable worth and equal pay.

The lines about a "cockamamie" idea, about "looney-tunes," have gotten out there far more than the fight for justice, and that's why I think it's time to raise hell, to spread the word, to organize women. Because there's no question in my mind but that rights are never won unless people are willing to fight for them.

In 1848, some women and men met in a very, very small little town, Seneca Falls, and they wrote a Declaration of Human Sentiments. The Declaration of Human Sentiments was modeled after our own Declaration of Independence, and it was very, very, simple. They said, "We hold these truths to be self-evident, that all men and women are created equal. That they are endowed by their Creator with certain inalienable rights, and among these are life, liberty, and the pursuit of happiness." I think it's time for the feminist movement, for the progressive movement, to review history and declare their own independence. It is time that we stop thinking about what is fashionable and what is not fashionable in this city, what's in and what is not in. I am told that when I say it's time to go into the streets these are the politics of the '60s.

The politics of the '60s . . . you know we could have one decade, those of us who are concerned about human rights in this century, but God forbid if we take a little more. We can have that little decade. But, when we're trying to fight to make sure that there is forward movement, and progress, and that the great gains of the civil rights decade of the '60s are not lost, then we are told that we are passé.

We want to use terms like equal opportunity employer, but we don't want them to mean anything. We want to just feel good. Well, the job of a person fighting for equality is not to make anybody feel good while there's injustice in our system, but to make us all uncomfortable.

The right wing, I feel, is being given a honeymoon, an outrageous honeymoon. Jerry Falwell just took a whirlwind, five-day trip to South Africa in the pursuit of the myth of the happy slave. Jerry Falwell went there and, no question about it, he found a few blacks who didn't agree with Bishop Tutu. In fact, he could once again pursue the classic defense of injustice, by justifying no change or ever-so-imperceptively-small change, on the basis that change will hurt the victims of injustice.

Well, we know that there was a huge uproar over Jerry Falwell's trip. His thinly veiled racism was seen by many of us for what it was. But that thinly veiled racism and, in my opinion, sexism, is running rampant in this country, and we are hardly questioning it.

In reviewing all the articles about what the president is going to do about the sanctions, we constantly see that little phrase, "He'll veto it if he thinks it will hurt the blacks." The only time we ever care about what the victims of injustice think is when we try to change the injustice itself.

After 15 years of fighting for women's equality, the only time I'm ever asked what women think is when I'm asked, "Mrs. Smeal (and they do generally say 'Mrs.'), how many women agree with you anyway?" And invariably, as we march down the street, some woman is interviewed who thinks we're all nuts. She thinks it's just perfectly fine the way it is. And that's it. Dismiss it. If we don't represent huge numbers, if there's not an instant poll right now, whatever the injustice is, it's okay.

Look at what this three-judge panel did. They are very educated men. They ruled that you don't even have to deal with injustice as long as everybody else does the same thing. That's called the free market system. You get away with discrimination if everybody else practices discrimination. Justifying the injustice.

We have a lot of experience in justifying injustice. In fighting it, we have ever so little experience. We recall the great names who have fought injustice. But we make sure of one thing—that they're all dead. Well, there's a lot of us around and we've got a lot of kick left in us, and we intend to raise hell while we're still living. And I don't think we can overcome any too soon.

We are fighting, I believe, for fundamental liberty and justice in our lives. Look at the abortion issue—the right to determine when and if you're going to be pregnant—really, the right to survive. Oh, I do love the great intellectual questions, such as, "Does a fertilized egg have more rights than I do?"

You know, I'm not debating that very much. I can't get over the fact that most people who want to debate this question are men. I'm not a sexist, and I generally do not call attention to the sex of my opposition, but I can't help noticing that most of the people picketing abortion clinics also are males. The Jerry Falwells, the Jesse Helmses, the Orrin Hatches—they never will have to face this decision. But we do.

I feel, without question, that we are dealing with life and death, that women have a right for their lives and their opportunities. And more importantly, every person on the face of this earth has an obligation to make her or his own decisions that impact on her or his own life.

Right now we are, I think, abandoning one of the great principles of our country: freedom of religion. The Pope has just visited Kenya and he said to that starving nation that birth control is wrong, a country whose average size of family is seven, that is racked by starvation. You know, in the sub-Saharan Desert area, nine million people will starve this year and 150 million people are at different levels of starvation. The average age of death is four. And he preaches no birth control.

We hardly can feed the people we have, and he preaches no birth control. That message is not just a message for Kenya. That message is having world-wide impact, and it's having an impact right here in this country.

The fight to outlaw abortion is fundamentally an attack on birth control. Let there be no mistake about that. It's fundamentally an attack on freedom of religion, and it's fundamentally an attack on a woman's right to her life and her pursuit of happiness.

I believe that every woman and every man who cares about a quality of life worth fighting for had better stand up, while they can still stand up, and join with us in a fight to keep abortion and birth control safe and legal. That's why I am organizing a mass mobilization in the spring of 1986 for abortion and birth control. I hope hundreds of thousands of people come here to Washington, but that will be only the first of many marches and many acts.

You know, there are a lot of people who want to advise us, who think we should operate only within the system of passing laws and getting Supreme Court decisions. Well, we did that with abortion. There is a Supreme Court decision that legalizes it, and, as you know, the opposition is not accepting that ruling as permanent. They are mobilizing. They are in the streets. They are threatening life and safety. They are using the tactics of the '60s in 1985. They're using tactics that they claim are those of civil rights (violent and non-violent), and they're fighting for what they believe in. They are very loud for a very small minority. Those of us who believe that women have the right to birth control and abortion must fight back. The Supreme Court alone cannot stand and defend the fundamental rights of people.

Thomas Jefferson once said that "the price of liberty is eternal vigilance." We also must be prepared to march, prepared to fight, and prepared to defend our liberty. We also must be prepared to fight to expand our liberties. We cannot just fight for the gains of yesteryear. We must fight for full equality.

The fight for the Equal Rights Amendment, I am told, is something we should give up. Well, we're not about to give it up. We're not about to give it up because we have a job to complete and the dream of full equality for all women to fulfill. The case-by-case approach is intolerable. Full equality is essential. But, if we don't fight for the dream of full equality, we will watch it be eroded statute-by-statute and case-by-case. So, we are going to make sure that we mount a campaign, this time at the state level in Vermont that will show that, indeed, there is plenty of fight left in the Equal Rights Amendment.

When the suffragists were stopped at the state level, they went to the federal level. And when they were stopped at the federal level, they went back to the state level. And they kept it up. For 56 state referendum campaigns, 480 legislative campaigns, 470 state constitutional campaigns, 277 state party campaigns, 30 national party conventions, 19 campaigns, and 19 successive Congresses, they kept it up. They kept it up until suffrage was theirs. And I believe we must keep it up, and keep it up, until equality is ours.

And I don't think we should step back from any hard or tough question. The opposition has a way of throwing every issue of the day at us, and a way of pretending that they are the only righteous people on this earth.

They claim we are the destroyers of the family, that we are the people without morals, and without concerns for the future. They make claims such as, "ERA leads to AIDS." They try to make this great connection. And we either laugh, because we don't know what to do with it, or we avoid the issue. I say it's time to stop avoiding these issues. They're not joking matters.

The right wing has a way of always singling out some class of people in our society and making them the untouchables, claiming God's wrath is upon them. They teach bigotry and hate, and we've got to recognize that for what it is. When they say ERA leads to AIDS, they are going after an oppressed class of people, lesbians and gay men. They are spreading ignorance and hate that could lead to the demise of all of us, because this is a dreadful disease that is spreading throughout the population of the world.

We are proud of fighting for the liberty of all people, and we are proud that we fight for gay and lesbian rights. We won't allow this issue to be distorted or to be used against women's equality. We won't step back from any issue. We will recognize bigotry for what it is, wherever it raises its ugly head. And we intend to wrap it around the neck of the right wing as we fight for liberty and justice for all.

I feel that one of the biggest problems that we have is that we haven't taken the right wing, fascist opposition seriously enough. In 1957 to 1961, I was at Duke University. I didn't know very much about the South. I was raised along the Great Lakes, around Erie, Pennsylvania. When I went to college, I decided to go to Duke. I didn't know that it was segregated. I had read about segregation, but I didn't know what it meant. I was first generation Italian-American. I could tell you all about discrimination against Italians, but I didn't know very much about discrimination against black people in the South.

But I got a crash course. Before you knew it, I was on the picket line at some movie theater in downtown Durham. It outraged me that black people were only allowed to sit in the unairconditioned balcony. So, when they asked for volunteers, I ended up there. The thing I will never forget is being called a "nigger-lover" and being spat on, because I believed people had a right to sit anywhere they wanted when they bought a ticket. I couldn't get over that hatred. I couldn't get over what made them think it was all right to call me such names.

The reason I bring this up now is because we're about to fight all over again unless we make a stand today. The Civil Rights Restoration Act is in Congress, and it's being tied up by all kinds of amendments. It's being called an abortion issue.

You know, when they want to kill something these days that deals with civil rights or women's rights, they slap on an abortion amendment. They make it an abortion issue. The great Civil Rights Act of 1964 is in trouble. Title IX for educational rights for women is in trouble. The Older American Discrimination Act is in trouble as well as protection for the physically disabled. Why? Because the Supreme Court and the Reagan administration have ruled that the federal government can fund discrimination. We're about to see the unraveling of all the gains of the last 30 and 40 years.

Well, there's no way we're going backwards.

We're going to launch an emergency campaign to save the Civil Rights Act, and I don't want to hear any American praise

Martin Luther King or any other great civil rights leader if that person isn't doing anything to save the Civil Rights Act in 1985. It's time to show where you stand today, not to recall the great triumphs for human progress of yesterday. I want to see a campaign that will stir the soul of this country again for justice.

I don't want to hear that we don't have idealism in this country, that the young kids only are interested in the almighty dollar and don't really care about the fight for equality and justice. I believe they do, so we're launching a campus campaign to save the Civil Rights Restoration Act, to save women's rights, and to move forward.

There's a movie out now called "Back to the Future." I can't say I'm a movie buff, but I think it's about time we went back to the business of the future of this country and stopped romanticizing the eighteenth and nineteenth centuries. We must look to the future of this nation and work to make this world safe for justice.

I also believe that we're on the verge of a major comeback in the women's movement. You should know that, according to a Lou Harris survey, 43% of the American people believe we have just begun. Now, there's one American who I don't quote much, but there's one thing on which I agree with him: "You ain't seen nothing yet."

We've just begun. We are going to lead a movement that will be big enough, and proud enough, to do justice to the dream of equality for all people.

ARE WOMEN'S VIEWS DIFFERENT?[1]

BETTY BUMPERS[2]

In 1982, Betty Bumpers founded Peace Links, an organization dedicated to reaching and involving mainstream, grass roots citizens in activities to reduce the threat of nuclear war. Since then, membership in the organization has grown to include 40,000 citizens in 40 states. Mrs. Bumpers, who is married to Senator Dale Bumpers of Arkansas, has been joined by more than 100 bipartisan congressional wives in her crusade to

[1]Delivered at a luncheon meeting at the fourth annual Women's Leadership Conference on Defense Issues, sponsored by the Committee for National Security, Marvin Center, George Washington University, June 15, 1985, noon to 2:00 P.M..

[2]For biographical note, see Appendix.

involve women in the peace issue. Nina Totenberg described the organization and its members:

> The women who have organized Peace Links are mainly Middle Americans with little or no history of political activism. Most still live the lives of a Norman Rockwell poster. What brought them out of the closet of political dormancy was the fear that their children would be exterminated in a nuclear war. . . . Betty Bumpers' idea when she started Peace Links was that democracy won't work unless everyday people get involved and make it clear what they want. "The premise of Peace Links is that women's voices must be heard," says Mrs. Bumpers. "The beauty of Peace Links is that it doesn't tell you what to do. It just gives you information . . . you make the decision about what you want to do." (*Parade Magazine*, March 2, 1986, p. 2)

On June 15, 1985, Mrs. Bumpers addressed the fourth annual Women's Leadership Conference on Defense Issues, sponsored by the Committee for National Security, in Washington, D. C. Her audience consisted of approximately 300 women leaders from 32 states.

In her speech, Mrs. Bumpers discussed the reasons why she organized Peace Links:

> When I founded Peace Links, I know I did so out of an instinct or an experience that was distinctly female. From the many women I talked to, I sensed that women were tuned into the potential disaster nuclear weapons posed, and understood the jeopardy their families constantly lived under in the name of "protection." I definitely believe that on the whole, women much more readily accept the notion that nuclear weapons cannot protect us without threatening our own survival.

In support of her thesis that women's views regarding war are different, Mrs. Bumpers drew from history (the observations of the first congresswoman, Jeanette Rankin, and Eleanor Roosevelt), public opinion surveys, a current study on women's attitudes by Carol Gilligan, and letters and conversations of "ordinary people" who were fearful about the likelihood of nuclear devastation. These sources led Mrs. Bumpers to conclude that

> This is a time in history when women's voices must be heard, or forever silenced. It's not because we think better than men, but we think differently. It's not women against men, but women *and* men. It's not that the world would have been better if women had run it, but that the world will *be better* when we as women, who bring our own perspective, share in running it.

Betty Bumpers's speech: When I founded Peace Links, I know I did so out of an instinct or an experience that was distinctly female. From the many women I talked to, I sensed that women were tuned into the potential disaster nuclear weapons posed, and understood the jeopardy their families constantly lived under in the name of "protection." I definitely believe that, on the whole, women much more readily accept the notion that nuclear weapons cannot protect us without threatening our own survival. And for that reason, women are ready and eager to pursue alternative ways of dealing with the international conflicts which will always occur.

Perhaps women view nuclear weapons differently because, historically, our lives have been structured differently from men's. We women have had the privilege of knowing we were *not* going to be called upon to don fatigues, helmets, and guns to fight wars as men are called upon to do. We have had the option of believing there could be other ways to resolve conflicts since we were not raised to respond to martial music and battle cries like men. In fact, we have not only had the option of believing conflicts could be resolved in other ways, we have had the practice of solving problems differently. Traditionally women have been taught to share, to provide for others, and to nurture and resolve whatever problems arose without physical violence.

This difference has not made women less patriotic or less brave. Women have historically put themselves in situations as risky as men in wartime as nurses, medics, and clerical staff; and many women continue to seek various ways to serve their country. Patriotism runs as deeply in women's veins as it does in men's, but it frequently gets expressed in different ways.

We can look to some animal species for some parallels. Female animals are not pacifists; they fight with great skill and ferocity, but they fight only to provide food and to protect their young. Unlike male animals, most female animals do not fight to establish dominance, or for strutting and glory.

It is interesting to note that the women's suffrage movement and the women's peace movement had many of the same origins. One of the reasons women sought the right to vote was because women believed their views were different and important, and many women sought the chance to help make policy that would keep our nation out of wars. In turn of the century women's suffrage literature and letters, it is easy to find expressed the sentiment that, "Once we get the right to vote, then we can ban the bullet." Jeanette Rankin was the first woman elected to Congress. She was elected from Montana in 1916, after women in Montana had the right to vote but before ratification of the 20th Amendment. The first vote she cast, and the one she personally considered most significant, was to vote against entry into World War I. She did so *not* without a great deal of thought and agony, and *not* without a great deal of pressure from other feminists who wanted her to cast her vote for war so women would not be perceived as weak. But Ms. Rankin voted her conscience. Later in reflecting on that vote, which cost her the next election, she said, "I have always felt there was great significance in the fact that the first woman who was ever asked what she thought about war voted no." As she said at the time she cast her historic vote, "Small use it will be to save democracy for the race if we cannot save the race for democracy." Those words ring so true today.

In 1933, Eleanor Roosevelt wrote a book entitled, *It's Up To The Women*. This book contains a chapter entitled, "Women and Peace," where, more than 50 years ago, Mrs. Roosevelt wrote:

> One of the things in which women are vitally interested today is the abolition of war as a means of settling disputes between nations, and I feel that this is particularly a question which is up to the women. Over and over again have I sat and listened to men talking since the close of the World War (this was of course World War I) and almost invariably they will voice the sentiment that it would be a fine thing if we never again needed to resort to war, but that human nature is so made that men will always feel that they must fight. This seems to be the instinctive reaction of most men. I find amongst many of the men who actually fought in the last war a very distinct feeling of the futility and waste, a real horror of the cruelty and filth, coupled with a firm decision that nothing will again drag them into the trenches of modern warfare. In the younger generation, however, there is still a lure in the martial music and flags flying and the mere adventure which any great risk holds for youth. . . .
>
> As I see it there are two things which women must do. One is to create a will to peace in all things, and the other is to make adventurous some other things in life besides war.

Mrs. Roosevelt concludes her chapter by saying that creating a world where we use greater ingenuity to solve problems has the possibilities of adventure and excitement and should take the place of the old glamour surrounding war. She maintains that the men will follow, but the women will have to lead the way.

Public opinion polls during the last several years have demonstrated what analysts refer to as the "gender gap." While women's views differ from men's on a number of issues, there has been a substantial difference between men's and women's views on war/peace issues. While it can be argued that the gender gap did not affect the outcome of the presidential election in 1984, polls continue to substantiate my personal findings from talking with women around the country that women see nuclear arms issues in a different framework than most men do.

In her book, *In a Different Voice*, Carol Gilligan has described what she has found as different perspectives on life held by women and men, as well as a difference in the way the two sexes resolve moral problems. Her findings indicate that women operate on an "ethic of care" and the inter-dependence of human beings as well as each person's responsibilities to others. Men, on the other hand, rely on a "justice" approach and on each person's right to be protected from the interference of others. I understand Carol Gilligan's findings, because I see them everyday when I speak to groups of women and men about nuclear arms. When focused on the issue, women immediately see the jeopardy we place our families, and families across the world, in when we attempt to protect ourselves and our rights by nuclear weapons. Women want to find safer ways to protect themselves and their families and to preserve life on this planet. Men continue to talk about building stronger and more powerful weapons because they are focused on protecting their rights instead of protecting human survival.

Admiral Gene Laroque has long been a supporter of Peace Links and our efforts to involve more women in the discussion and policy decisions regarding national security and nuclear weapons. About a year ago he said to me,

> Betty, I've always believed you were on to something going after the women on this issue, and I think I've figured out why. Working with men over the years I have come to realize that when it comes to a problem, men want to define it, and re-define it. They turn the problem inside and out, and up and down. Men spend all their time focused on the problem. Something my wife said the other night made me realize that when women deal with a problem, they start immediately trying to solve it. That's why we need women to get involved now. We need to spend more time focused on what the solution to the nuclear dilemma is, and less time hung-up on the problems.

One of the realizations my work with Peace Links has brought to me is that women have felt powerless and shut-out of a system that is making decisions to protect its citizens by methods that threaten our own destruction. Some of my personal goals are to:

1. help women learn how to become part of this democracy's policymaking, and
2. help them assume some of the citizen's responsibility for our policies, and
3. to teach citizenship to their children.

This is important because women who become mothers today are taking a big risk. Just last week I spoke with a young woman working on a story for *Newsweek* about people's divergent views on the nuclear arms race. She called me full of despair and hopelessness, and said to me, "Should I even consider having a baby?" Every time this question comes up, I find myself taken aback that motherhood as so many of us have enjoyed it and taken it for granted as a natural part of life, should provide a dilemma to young women who wonder whether they even have the right to bring another life into such an unsafe world. I told her she ought to have a baby, not only because otherwise she would miss all the joys, but also because it will redouble her commitment to ending the threat of nuclear war. Mothers like her will not consent to raising their children under the nuclear shadow. And, what hope for the future do we have if not a *new generation* who is raised by mothers and fathers who understand the futility of trying to protect ourselves by the suicide that use of nuclear weapons would almost invariably mean? The hope of our world lies in a new generation who is raised with the realization that with nuclear weapons we went too far and built weapons we could no longer use, and that new ways of resolving conflict are necessary. It is the new generation who can help us come up with 21st century solutions to our problems.

This is a time in history when women's voices must be heard, or forever silenced. It's not because we think better than men, but we think differently. It's not women against men, but women *and* men. It's not that the world would have been better if women had run it, but that the world will *be better* when we as women, who bring our own perspective, share in running it.

Do you believe that if women were called upon to make choices that they would choose to put our dollars into weapons of destruction which will become quickly obsolete, or into nurturing and educating strong and healthy minds which will become a national treasure for a lifetime and which will help us work our way out of this dilemma? If women were given the choice, do you believe they would, in light of the four major academies that exist in this country in addition to our universities, where our best and brightest are recruited to learn the "arts of war" also choose to create academies which our best and brightest can attend to learn the "arts of peace"?

Women's views are different, and that's why it's important women become part of the dialogue on this issue at all levels. That's why Peace Links and other organizations are providing women the information and encouragement they need to trust their instincts and speak out on this issue. Women need to learn to trust the value system we've learned in this democracy and to trust ourselves and our perspective enough to speak out and help our elected leadership make these decisions. Traveling across this country for three years, I have found that women are ready for new solutions; now we must be ready to help lead the way.

One of the first letters I received after founding Peace Links was sent to me by a woman from Canada. Her letter has stayed with me, and sometimes when I've just about had it with working for peace, I remember her words:

> A simple day with the dog barking at the mailman, the kids getting off the school bus, watching the sun from my kitchen windows as I wash the supper dishes . . . could easily be turned into horrific days filled with radiation sickness, contaminated food supplies and no mail at all!
> I have often thought of myself as descending from a long line of ancestors who were strong enough to survive the history of the world. I would like to leave this world some day with the feeling that in ten or fifty or a hundred generations from now, a many times great-granddaughter of mine will feel the same way . . . only she will know that she came from a generation of ancestors who took control of the world and saved it for the future.

INTERPRETING THE CONSTITUTION

ADDRESS TO THE AMERICAN BAR ASSOCIATION[1]

EDWIN MEESE III[2]

It is not uncommon for the American Bar Association to invite the attorney general of the United States and members of the Supreme Court to address the ABA at its annual meeting, but it *is* unusual for these speeches to inspire the kind of debate that followed Attorney General Edwin Meese III's address to the association's House of Delegates on July 9, 1985. Meese's remarks attracted only perfunctory attention and press coverage at the time of their delivery; however, subsequent speeches by two Supreme Court justices spiralled his words into the national limelight [see p. 76 for Justice William J. Brennan, Jr.'s address]. Stuart Taylor, Jr., writing in the *New York Times*, observed that

> recent history has seen nothing quite like the rhetorical crossfire between Attorney General Edwin Meese III and two members of the Supreme Court. Speeches by Associate Justices John Paul Stevens last week [October 23, 1985] and William J. Brennan, Jr., on October 12, dramatized the concern provoked in the Court's marble edifice by the Administration's drive to change the course of constitutional law.
>
> Since the defeat of Franklin D. Roosevelt's court-packing plan in 1937, it has been rare for top executive branch officials to assail the Supreme Court directly. And it has been virtually unheard of for members of the Court off the bench to criticize the constitutional views of top executive branch officials. Because much of the Court's authority rests on its appearance of Olympian detachment and impartiality, Justices have traditionally been wary of debate on politically charged issues. This tradition is eroding. (October 28, 1985, p. 10)

Meese has been a loyal supporter of Ronald Reagan for more than 20 years. He served under Reagan when he was governor of California and has been an influential counselor of the president in Washington. His appointment as attorney general had been approved only three months before, after lengthy hearings involving charges of influence peddling, when Meese chose the bar association meeting for his first major statement about the Supreme Court. Some observers interpreted the attorney general's speech as the opening salvo in an attack by the Reagan Administration on the Court's lack of support for its conservative ideology. The

[1]Delivered to the annual meeting of the House of Delegates of the American Bar Association, Sheraton Washington Hotel, Washington, D.C., 10:30 A.M., July 9, 1985. Reprinted with the permission of the United States Justice Department.

[2]For biographical note, see Appendix.

statement that provoked controversy was Meese's claim that "far too many of the Court's opinions, on the whole, have been more policy choices than articulations of long-term constitutional principle." Denouncing major Supreme Court rulings of the last 60 years, Meese called upon judges to look to "the original meaning of constitutional provisions" as "the only reliable guide for judgment." According to Stuart Taylor, Jr., "No attorney general in the past four decades has set out so deliberately to reduce the power of the judiciary or to screen the ideological credentials of new appointees. Champions of liberal judicial activism have launched a ferocious counterattack" (*New Republic*, January 6 & 13, 1986, p. 17).

A profile in *Newsweek* (April 2, 1984, p. 24) described him as "genial" and observed that "he promotes collegial harmony and he keeps cool under pressure. . . . he remains at heart an all-round amiable fellow."

Reporters noted that, at the last minute, Meese altered his remarks to the bar association, omitting some of the more forceful criticisms contained in his prepared text, perhaps an indication that he was not ready to attack the Court as emphatically as some of his aides and speechwriters would have liked. Specifically, he omitted the remark, "Nowhere else has the principle of federalism been dealt so politically violent and constitutionally suspect a blow as by the theory of incorporation," and the assertion, "In my opinion a drift back toward the radical egalitarianism and expansive civil libertarianism of the Warren Court would once again be a threat to the notion of limited but energetic government." (These passages have been bracketed and italicized in the following text to indicate that they were not actually said.)

Edwin Meese III's speech: Welcome to our Federal City. It is an honor to be here today to address the House of Delegates of the American Bar Association. I know the sessions here and those next week in London will be very productive.

It is, of course, entirely fitting that we lawyers gather here in this home of our government. We Americans, after all, rightly pride ourselves on having produced the greatest political wonder of the world: a government of laws and not of men. Thomas Paine was right: "America has no monarch: Here the law is king."

Perhaps nothing underscores Paine's assessment quite as much as the eager anticipation with which Americans await the conclusion of the term of the Supreme Court. Lawyers and laymen alike regard the Court not so much with awe as with a healthy respect. The law matters here and the business of our highest court, the subject of my remarks today, is crucially important to our political order.

At this time of year I'm always reminded of how utterly unpredictable the Court can be in rendering its judgments. Several years ago, for example, there was quite a controversial case, *TVA* v. *Hill*. This dispute involved the EPA and the now-legendary snail darter, a creature of curious purpose and forgotten origins. In any event, when the case was handed down, one publication announced that there was some good news and some bad news. The bad news in their view was that the snail darter had won; the good news was that he didn't use the 14th Amendment.

Once again, the Court has finished a term characterized by a nearly crushing workload. There were 4,935 cases on the docket this year; 179 cases were granted review; 140 cases issued in signed opinions; 11 were *per curiam* rulings. Such a docket lends credence to Tocqueville's assessment that, in America, every political question seems sooner or later to become a legal question. (I won't even mention the statistics of the lower federal courts; let's just say I think we'll all be in business for quite a while.)

In looking back over the work of the Court, I am again struck by how little the statistics tell us about the true role of the Court. In reviewing a term of the Court, it is important to take a moment and reflect upon the proper role of the Supreme Court in our constitutional system.

The intended role of the judiciary generally and the Supreme Court in particular was to serve as the "bulwarks of a limited constitution." The judges, the Founders believed, would not fail to regard the Constitution as "fundamental law" and would "regulate their decisions" by it. As the "faithful guardians of the Constitution," the judges were expected to resist any political effort to depart from the literal provisions of the Constitution. The text of the document and the original intention of those who framed it would be the judicial standard in giving effect to the Constitution.

You will recall that Alexander Hamilton, defending the federal courts to be created by the new Constitution, remarked that the want of a judicial power under the Articles of Confederation had been the crowning defect of that first effort at a national constitution. Ever the consummate lawyer, Hamilton pointed out that "laws are a dead letter without courts to expound and define their true meaning."

The anti-federalist *Brutus* took him to task in the New York press for what the critics of the Constitution considered his naivete. That prompted Hamilton to write his classic defense of judicial power in *The Federalist*, No. 78.

An independent judiciary under the Constitution, he said, would prove to be the "citadel of public justice and the public security." Courts were "peculiarly essential in a limited constitution." Without them, there would be no security against "the encroachments and oppressions of the representative body," no protection against "unjust and partial" laws.

Hamilton, like his colleague Madison, knew that *all* political power is "of an encroaching nature." In order to keep the powers created by the Constitution within the boundaries marked out by the Constitution, an independent—but constitutionally bound—judiciary was essential. The purpose of the Constitution, after all, was the creation of limited but also energetic government, institutions with the power to govern, but also with structures to keep the power in check. As Madison put it, the Constitution enabled the government to control the governed, but also obliged it to control itself.

But even beyond the institutional role, the Court serves the American republic in yet another, more subtle way. The problem of any popular government, of course, is seeing to it that the people obey the laws. There are but two ways: either by physical force or by moral force. In many ways the Court remains the primary moral force in American politics.

Tocqueville put it best:

> The great object of justice is to substitute the idea of right for that of violence, to put intermediaries between the government and the use of its physical force. . . .
> It is something astonishing what authority is accorded to the intervention of a court of justice by the general opinion of mankind. . . .
> The moral force in which tribunals are clothed makes the use of physical force infinitely rarer, for in most cases it takes its place; and when finally physical force is required, its power is doubled by this moral authority.

By fulfilling its proper function, the Supreme Court contributes both to institutional checks and balances and to the moral undergirding of the entire constitutional edifice. For the Supreme Court is the only national institution that daily grapples with the most fundamental political questions and defends them with written expositions. Nothing less would serve to perpetuate the sanctity of the rule of law so effectively.

But that is not to suggest that the justices are a body of Platonic guardians. Far from it. The Court is what it was understood to be when the Constitution was framed: a political body. The judicial process is, at its most fundamental level, a political process. While not a partisan political process, it is political in the truest sense of that word. It is a process wherein public deliberations occur over what constitutes the common good under the terms of a written constitution.

As a result, as Benjamin Cardozo pointed out, "the great tides and currents which engulf the rest of men do not turn aside in their course and pass the judges by." Granting that, Tocqueville knew what was required.

As he wrote:

> The federal judges therefore must not only be good citizens and men of education and integrity, . . . [they] must also be statesmen; they must know how to understand the spirit of the age, to confront those obstacles that can be overcome, and to steer out of the current when the tide threatens to carry them away, and with them the sovereignty of the union and obedience to its laws.

On that confident note, let's consider the Court's work this past year.

As has been generally true in recent years, the 1984 term did not yield a coherent set of decisions. Rather, it seemed to produce what one commentator has called a "jurisprudence of idiosyncracy." Taken as a whole, the work of the term defies analysis by any strict standard. It is neither simply liberal nor simply conservative; neither simply activist nor simply restrained; neither simply principled nor simply partisan. The Court this term continued to roam at large in a veritable constitutional forest.

I believe, however, that there are at least three general areas that merit close scrutiny: federalism, criminal law, and freedom of religion.

In *Garcia* v. *San Antonio Metropolitan Transit Authority*, the Court displayed what was in the view of this Administration an inaccurate reading of the text of the Constitution and a disregard for the Framers' intention that state and local governments be a buffer against the centralizing tendencies of the national Leviathan. Specifically, five Justices denied that the Tenth Amendment protects states from federal laws regulating the wages and hours of state or local employees. Thus the Court overruled, but barely, a contrary holding in *National League of Cities* v. *Usery*. We hope for a day when the Court returns to the basic principles of the Constitution as expressed in *Usery*; such instability in decisions concerning the fundamental principle of federalism does our Constitution no service.

Meanwhile, the constitutional status of the states further suffered as the Court curbed state power to regulate the economy, notably the professions. In *Metropolitan Life Insurance Co.* v. *Ward*, the Court used the Equal Protection Clause to spear an Alabama insurance tax on gross premiums preferring in-state companies over out-of-state rivals. In *New Hampshire* v. *Piper*, the Court held that the Privileges and Immunities Clause of Article IV barred New Hampshire from completely excluding a nonresident from admission to its bar. With the apparent policy objective of creating unfettered national markets for occupations before its eyes, the Court unleashed Article IV against any state preference for residents involving the professions or service industries. *Hicklin* v. *Orbeck* and *Baldwin* v. *Montana Fish and Game Commission* are illustrative.

On the other hand, we gratefully acknowledge the respect shown by the Court for state and local sovereignty in a number of cases, including *Atascadero State Hospital* v. *Scanlon*.

In *Atascadero*, a case involving violations of §504 of Rehabilitation Act of 1973, the Court honored the Eleventh Amendment in limiting private damage suits against states. Congress, it said, must express its intent to expose states to liability affirmatively and clearly.

In *Town of Haile* v. *City of Eau Claire*, the Court found that active state supervision of municipal activity was not required to cloak municipalities with immunity under the Sherman Act. And, states were judged able to confer Sherman Act immunity upon private parties in *Southern Motor Carrier Rate Conference* v. *U.S.* They must, said the Court, clearly articulate and affirmatively express a policy to displace competition with compelling anticompetitive action so long as the private action is actively supervised by the state.

And, in *Oklahoma City* v. *Tuttle*, the Court held that a single incident of unconstitutional and egregious police misconduct is insufficient to support a Section 1983 action against municipalities for allegedly inadequate police training or supervision.

Our view is that federalism is one of the most basic principles of our Constitution. By allowing the states sovereignty sufficient to govern we better secure our ultimate goal of political liberty through decentralized government. We do not advocate states' rights; we advocate states' responsibilities. We need to remember that state and local governments are not inevitably abusive of rights. It was, after all, at the turn of the century the states that were the laboratories of social and economic progress—and the federal courts that blocked their way. We believe that there is a proper constitutional sphere for state governance under our scheme of limited, popular government.

Recognizing, perhaps, that the nation is in the throes of a drug epidemic which has severely increased the burden borne by law enforcement officers, the Court took a more progressive stance on the Fourth Amendment, undoing some of the damage previously done by its piecemeal incorporation through the Fourteenth Amendment. Advancing from its landmark *Leon* decision in 1984 which created a good-faith exception to the Exclusionary Rule when a flawed warrant is obtained by police, the Court permitted warrantless searches under certain limited circumstances.

The most prominent among these Fourth Amendment cases were:

New Jersey v. *T.L.O.*, which upheld warrantless searches of public school students based on reasonable suspicion that a law or school rule has been violated; this also restored a clear local authority over another problem in our society, school discipline;

California v. *Carney*, which upheld the warrantless search of a mobile home;

U.S. v. *Sharpe*, which approved on-the-spot detention of a suspect for preliminary questioning and investigation;

U.S. v. *Johns*, upholding the warrantless search of sealed packages in a car several days after their removal by police who possessed probable cause to believe the vehicle contained contraband;

U.S. v. *Hensley*, which permitted a warrantless investigatory stop based on an unsworn flyer from a neighboring police department which possessed reasonable suspicion that the detainee was a felon;

Hayes v. *Florida*, which tacitly endorsed warrantless seizures in the field for the purpose of fingerprinting based on reasonable suspicion of criminal activity;

U.S. v. *Hernandez*, which upheld border detentions and warrantless searches by customs officials based on reasonable suspicion of criminal activity.

Similarly, the Court took steps this term to place the *Miranda* ruling in proper perspective, stressing its origin in the court rather than in the Constitution. In *Oregon* v. *Elstad*, the Court held that failure to administer *Miranda* warnings and the consequent receipt of a confession ordinarily will not taint a second confession after *Miranda* warnings are received.

The enforcement of criminal law remains one of our most important efforts. It is crucial that the state and local authorities, from the police to the prosecutors, be able to combat the growing tide of crime effectively. Toward that end we advocate a due regard for the rights of the accused, but also a due regard for the keeping of the public peace and the safety and happiness of the people. We will continue to press for a proper scope for the rules of exclusion, lest truth in the fact finding process be allowed to suffer.

I have mentioned the areas of federalism and criminal law; now I will turn to the religion cases.

Most probably, this term will be best remembered for the decisions concerning the Establishment Clause of the First Amendment. The Court continued to apply its standard three-pronged test. Four cases merit mention.

In the first, *City of Grand Rapids* v. *Ball*, the Court nullified Shared Time and Community Education programs offered within parochial schools. Although the programs provided instruction in non-sectarian subjects, and were taught by full-time or part-time public school teachers, the Court nonetheless found that they promoted religion in three ways: the state-paid instructors might wittingly or unwittingly indoctrinate students; the symbolic union of church and state interest in state-provided instruction signaled support for religion; and, the programs in effect subsidized the religious functions of parochial schools by relieving them of responsibility for teaching some secular subjects. The symbolism test proposed in *Ball* precludes virtually any state assistance offered to parochial schools.

In *Aguilor* v. *Felton*, the Court invalidated a program of secular instruction for low-income students in sectarian schools, provided by public school teachers who were supervised to safeguard students against efforts of indoctrination.

With a bewildering Catch-22 logic, the Court declared that the supervisory safeguards at issue in the statute constituted unconstitutional government entanglement: "The religious school, which has as a primary purpose the advancement and preservation of a particular religion, must endure the ongoing presence of state personnel whose primary purpose is to monitor teachers and students in an attempt to guard against the infiltration of religious thought." Secretary of Education William Bennett has suggested such logic may reveal a "disdain" for education as well as religion.

In *Wallace* v. *Jaffree*, the Court said in essence that states may set aside time in public schools for meditation or reflection so long as the legislation does not stipulate that it be used for voluntary prayer. Of course, what the Court gave with one hand, it took back with the other; the Alabama moment of silence statute failed to pass muster.

In *Thornton* v. *Caldor*, a 7-2 majority overturned a state law prohibiting private employers from discharging an employee for refusing to work on his Sabbath. We hope that this does not mean that the Court is abandoning last term's first but tentative steps toward state accommodation of religion in the Creche case.

In trying to make sense of the religion cases, from whichever side, it is important to remember how this body of tangled caselaw came about. Most Americans forget that it was not until 1925, in *Gitlow* v. *New York*, that any provision of the Bill of Rights was applied to the states. Nor was it until 1947 that the Establishment Clause was made applicable to the states through the 14th Amendment. This is striking because the Bill of Rights, as debated, created, and ratified, was designed to apply only to the national government.

The Bill of Rights came about largely as the result of the demands of the critics of the new Constitution, the unfortunately misnamed Anti-Federalists. They feared, as George Mason of Virginia put it, that in time the national authority would "devour" the states. Since each state had a bill of rights, it was only appropriate that so powerful a national government as that created by the Constitution have one as well. Though Hamilton insisted a bill of rights was not necessary and even destructive, and Madison (at least at first) thought a bill of rights to be but a "parchment barrier" to political power, the Federalists agreed to add a bill of rights.

Though the first ten amendments that were ultimately ratified fell far short of what the Anti-Federalists desired, both Federalists and Anti-Federalists agreed that the amendments were a curb on national power.

When this view was questioned before the Supreme Court in *Barron* v. *Baltimore* (1833), Chief Justice Marshall wholeheartedly agreed. The Constitution said what it meant and meant what it said. Neither political expediency nor judicial desire was sufficient to change the clear import of the language of the Constitution. The Bill of Rights did not apply to the states—and, he said, that was that.

Until 1925, that is.

Since then a good portion of constitutional adjudication has been aimed at extending the scope of the doctrine of incorporation. But the most that can be done is to expand the scope; nothing can be done to shore up the intellectually shaky foundation upon which the doctrine rests. [*And nowhere else has the principle of federalism been dealt so politically violent and constitutionally suspect a blow as by the theory of incorporation.* (Included in preliminary release, but not actually said.)]

In thinking particularly of the use to which the First Amendment has been put in the area of religion, one finds much merit in Justice Rehnquist's recent dissent in *Jaffree*. "It is impossible," Justice Rehnquist argued, "to build sound constitutional doctrine upon a mistaken understanding of constitutional history." His conclusion was bluntly to the point: "If a constitutional theory has no basis in the history of the amendment it seeks to interpret, it is difficult to apply and yields unprincipled results."

The point, of course, is that the Establishment Clause of the First Amendment was designed to prohibit Congress from establishing a national church. The belief was that the Constitution should not allow Congress to designate a particular faith or sect as politically above the rest. But to have argued, as is popular today, that the amendment demands a strict neutrality between religion and irreligion would have struck the founding generation as bizarre. The purpose was to prohibit religious tyranny, not to undermine religion generally.

In considering these areas of adjudication—federalism, criminal law, and religion—it seems fair to conclude that far too many of the Court's opinions were, on the whole, more policy choices than articulations of constitutional principle. The voting blocs, the arguments, all reveal a greater allegiance to what the Court thinks constitutes sound public policy than a deference to what the Constitution, its text and intention, may demand.

It is also safe to say that until there emerges a coherent jurisprudential stance, the work of the Court will continue in this ad hoc fashion. But that is not to argue for *any* jurisprudence.

[*In my opinion a drift back toward the radical egalitarianism and expansive civil libertarianism of the Warren Court would once again be a threat to the notion of limited but energetic government.* (Included in preliminary release, but not actually said.)]

What, then, should a constitutional jurisprudence actually be? It should be a Jurisprudence of Original Intention. By seeking to judge policies in light of principles, rather than remold principles in light of policies, the Court could avoid both the charge of incoherence and the charge of being either too conservative or too liberal.

A jurisprudence seriously aimed at the explication of original intention would produce defensible principles of government that would not be tainted by ideological predilection.

This belief in a Jurisprudence of Original Intention also reflects a deeply rooted commitment to the idea of democracy. The Constitution represents the consent of the governed to the structures and powers of the government. The Constitution is the fundamental will of the people; that is why it is the fundamental law. To allow the courts to govern simply by what it views at the time as fair and decent, is a scheme of government no longer popular; the idea of democracy has suffered. The permanence of the Constitution has been weakened. A Constitution that is viewed as only what the judges say it is, is no longer a constitution in the true sense.

Those who framed the Constitution chose their words carefully; they debated at great length the most minute points. The language they chose meant something. It is incumbent upon the Court to determine what that meaning was. This is not a shockingly new theory; nor is it arcane or archaic.

Joseph Story, who was in a way a lawyer's Everyman—lawyer, justice, and teacher of law—had a theory of judging that merits reconsideration.

Though speaking specifically of the Constitution, his logic reaches to statutory construction as well.

> In construing the Constitution of the United States, we are in the first instance to consider, what are its nature and objects, its scope and design, as apparent from the structure of the instrument, viewed as a whole and also viewed in its component parts. Where its words are plain, clear and determinate, they require no interpretation. . . . Where the words admit of two senses, each of which is conformable to general usage, that sense is to be adopted, which without departing from the literal import of the words, best harmonizes with the nature and objects, the scope and design of the instrument.

A Jurisprudence of Original Intention would take seriously the admonition of Justice Story's friend and colleague, John Marshall, in *Marbury* that the Constitution is a limitation on judicial power as well as executive and legislative. That is what Chief Justice Marshall meant in *McCulloch* when he cautioned judges never to forget it is a constitution they are expounding.

It has been and will continue to be the policy of this administration to press for a Jurisprudence of Original Intention. In the cases we file and those we join as *amicus*, we will endeavor to resurrect the original meaning of constitutional provisions and statutes as the only reliable guide for judgment.

Within this context, let me reaffirm our commitment to pursuing the policies most necessary to public justice. We will continue our vigorous enforcement of civil rights laws; we will not rest till unlawful discrimination ceases. We will continue our all-out war on drugs: both supply and demand, both national and international in scope. We intend to bolster public safety by a persistent war on crime. We will endeavor to stem the growing tide of pornography and its attendant costs, sexual and child abuse. We will be battling the heretofore largely ignored legal cancer of white collar crime, and its cousin, defense procurement fraud. And finally, as we still reel as a people, I pledge to you our commitment to fight terrorism here and abroad. For as long as the innocent are fair prey for the barbarians of this world, civilization is not safe.

We will pursue our agenda within the context of our written Constitution of limited yet energetic powers. Our guide in every case will be the sanctity of the rule of law and the proper limits of governmental power.

It is our belief that only "the sense in which the Constitution was accepted and ratified by the nation," and only the sense in which laws were drafted and passed provide a solid foundation for adjudication. Any other standard suffers the defect of pouring new meaning into old words, thus creating new powers and new rights totally at odds with the logic of our Constitution and its commitment to the rule of law.

THE CONSTITUTION OF THE UNITED STATES: CONTEMPORARY RATIFICATION[1]

WILLIAM J. BRENNAN, JR.[2]

With the bicentennial of the signing of the Constitution of the United States on September 17, 1987, approaching and a commission at work on plans to celebrate it, a lively 1985 airing of views on constitutional interpretation by the Attorney General of the United States and two Supreme Court justices seemed to reveal more conflict than shared pride. The controversy began in July, when in a speech to the American Bar Association (see p. 64) Attorney General Edwin Meese III attacked several Supreme Court opinions as "bizarre," denounced many of the court rulings of the past sixty years, and called for judges to look to the "original meaning of constitutional provision" as "the only reliable guide for judgment." The confrontation which followed was described by Stuart Taylor, Jr., in the *New York Times* (see p. 64).

The first Supreme Court justice to discuss constitutional interpretation after Meese's ABA address was the oldest, most senior, and generally considered the most liberal court member, William J. Brennan, Jr. In his speech, Brennan argued that current justices do in fact "look to the history of the time of framing and to the intervening history of interpretation. But the ultimate question must be, what do the words of the text mean in our time."

The media generally interpreted Brennan's speech as a rebuttal of Meese's earlier remarks, noting, for example, that "Meese's speech drew a sharp and unusually direct retort" (*U.S. News and World Report,* January 13, 1986, p. 16) from Brennan, although he didn't mention the attorney general by name, "his comments were an unusual and unmistakably pointed rebuttal of views expressed in recent months by Attorney General Edwin Meese" (Stephen Wermiel, *Wall Street Journal*, October 14, 1985, p. 34), and "the immediate object of Justice Brennan's anger is quite obviously, Attorney General Edwin Meese III" (Walter Berns, *Wall Street Journal*, October 23, 1985, p. 32). However, in an article based on an interview with Justice Brennan, Stuart Taylor, Jr. reported in the *New York Times* that

> Justice Brennan declined to comment directly on the views of Mr. Meese, whom he termed "a very, very pleasant gentleman." He stressed that a speech he gave last October 12, rejecting the view widely associated with Mr. Meese that judges should precisely follow the original intentions of the Constitution's framers, "was not a response to anything the Attorney General had said." Accounts of the *New York Times* and other publications had suggested that the speech appeared to be an implicit criticism of Mr. Meese. But Justice Bren-

[1]Delivered at the Text and Teaching Symposium, Georgetown University, Washington, D.C., 9 A.M., October 12, 1985.

[2]For biographical note, see Appendix.

> nan took pains Monday to say that he had prepared his speech months before Mr. Meese began a public campaign last July to restore the framers' original meaning as "the only reliable guide" for constitutional interpretation. (April 16, 1986, p. 18)

Regardless of whether the two speeches actually constituted a debate—an exchange in which one side replies to another—they generated unusual media coverage. Leading newspapers, news magazines, and syndicated columnists not only reported the speeches, but also carried editorials and special articles on the controversy by judicial scholars and experts.

That a speech which attracted such widespread national attention was delivered by Justice Brennan to a symposium of about 200 educators in a university auditorium at 9:00 in the morning may surprise some readers. However, with advanced communications technology, public figures increasingly use academic forums to publicize their positions.

William J. Brennan, Jr.'s speech: I am deeply grateful for the invitation to participate in the "Text and Teaching" symposium. This rare opportunity to explore classic texts with participants of such wisdom, acumen and insight as those who have preceded and will follow me to this podium is indeed exhilarating. But it is also humbling. Even to approximate the standards of excellence of these vigorous and graceful intellects is a daunting task. I am honored that you have afforded me this opportunity to try.

It will perhaps not surprise you that the text I have chosen for exploration is the amended Constitution of the United States, which, of course, entrenches the Bill of Rights and the Civil War amendments, and draws sustenance from the bedrock principles of another great text, the Magna Carta. So fashioned, the Constitution embodies the aspiration to social justice, brotherhood, and human dignity that brought this nation into being. The Declaration of Independence, the Constitution and the Bill of Rights solemnly committed the United States to be a country where the dignity and rights of all persons were equal before all authority. In all candor we must concede that part of this egalitarianism in America has been more pretension than realized fact. But we are an aspiring people, a people with faith in progress. Our amended Constitution is the lodestar for our aspirations. Like every text worth reading, it is not crystalline. The phrasing is broad and the limitations of its provisions are not clearly marked. Its majestic generalities and ennobling pronouncements are both luminous and obscure. This ambiguity of course calls forth interpretation, the interaction of reader and text. The encounter with the Constitutional text has been, in many senses, my life's work.

My approach to this text may differ from the approach of other participants in this symposium to their texts. Yet such differences may themselves stimulate reflection about what it is we do when we "interpret" a text. Thus I will attempt to elucidate my approach to the text as well as my substantive interpretation.

Perhaps the foremost difference is the fact that my encounters with the constitutional text are not purely or even primarily introspective; the Constitution cannot be for me simply a contemplative haven for private moral reflection. My relation to this great text is inescapably public. That is not to say that my reading of the text is not a personal reading, only that the personal reading perforce occurs in a public context, and is open to critical scrutiny from all quarters.

The Constitution is fundamentally a public text—the monumental charter of a government and a people—and a Justice of the Supreme Court must apply it to resolve public controversies. For, from our beginnings, a most important consequence of the constitutionally created separation of powers has been the American habit, extraordinary to other democracies, of casting social, economic, philosophical and political questions in the form of law suits, in an attempt to secure ultimate resolution by the Supreme Court. In this way, important aspects of the most fundamental issues confronting our democracy may finally arrive in the Supreme Court for judicial determination. Not infrequently, these are the issues upon which contemporary society is most deeply divided. They arouse our deepest emotions. The main burden of my twenty-nine Terms on the Supreme Court has thus been to wrestle with the Constitution in this heightened public context, to draw meaning from the text in order to resolve public controversies.

Two other aspects of my relation to this text warrant mention. First, constitutional interpretation for a federal judge is, for the most part, obligatory. When litigants approach the bar of court to adjudicate a constitutional dispute, they may justifiably demand an answer. Judges cannot avoid a definitive interpretation because they feel unable to, or would prefer not to, penetrate to the full meaning of the Constitution's provisions. Unlike literary critics, judges cannot merely savor the tensions or revel in the ambiguities inhering in the text—judges must resolve them.

Second, consequences flow from a Justice's interpretation in a direct and immediate way. A judicial decision respecting the incompatibility of Jim Crow with a constitutional guarantee of equality is not simply a contemplative exercise in defining the shape of a just society. It is an order—supported by the full coercive power of the State—that the present society change in a fundamental aspect. Under such circumstances the process of deciding can be a lonely, troubling experience for fallible human beings conscious that their best may not be adequate to the challenge. We Justices are certainly aware that we are not final because we are infallible; we know that we are infallible only because we are final. One does not forget how much may depend on the decision. More than the litigants may be affected. The course of vital social, economic, and political currents may be directed.

These three defining characteristics of my relation to the constitutional text—its public nature, obligatory character, and consequentialist aspect—cannot help but influence the way I read that text. When Justices interpret the Constitution they speak for their community, not for themselves alone. The act of interpretation must be undertaken with full consciousness that it is, in a very real sense, the community's interpretation that is sought. Justices are not platonic guardians appointed to wield authority according to their personal moral predilections. Precisely because coercive force must attend any judicial decision to countermand the will of a contemporary majority, the Justices must render constitutional interpretations that are received as legitimate. The source of legitimacy is, of course, a wellspring of controversy in legal and political circles. At the core of the debate is what the late Yale Law School professor Alexander Bickel labeled "the counter-majoritarian difficulty." Our commitment to self-governance in a representative democracy must be reconciled with vesting in electorally unaccountable Justices the power to invalidate the expressed desires of representative bodies on the ground of inconsistency with higher law. Because judicial power resides in the authority to give meaning to the Constitution, the debate is really a debate about how to read the text, about constraints on what is legitimate interpretation.

There are those who find legitimacy in fidelity to what they call "the intentions of the Framers." In its most doctrinaire incarnation, this view demands that Justices discern exactly what the Framers thought about the question under consideration and simply follow that intention in resolving the case before them. It is a view that feigns self-effacing deference to the specific judgments of those who forged our original social compact. But in truth it is little more than arrogance cloaked as humility. It is arrogant to pretend that from our vantage we can gauge accurately the intent of the Framers on application of principle to specific, contemporary questions. All too often, sources of potential enlightenment such as records of the ratification debates provide sparse or ambiguous evidence of the original intention. Typically, all that can be gleaned is that the Framers themselves did not agree about the application or meaning of particular constitutional provisions, and hid their differences in cloaks of generality. Indeed, it is far from clear whose intention is relevant—that of the drafters, the congressional disputants, or the ratifiers in the states?—or even whether the idea of an original intention is a coherent way of thinking about a jointly drafted document drawing its authority from a general assent of the states. And apart from the problematic nature of the sources, our distance of two centuries cannot but work as a prism refracting all we perceive. One cannot help but speculate that the chorus of lamentations calling for interpretation faithful to "original intention"—and proposing nullification of interpretations that fail this quick litmus test—must inevitably come from persons who have no familiarity with the historical record.

Perhaps most importantly, while proponents of this facile historicism justify it as a depoliticization of the judiciary, the political underpinnings of such a choice should not escape notice. A position that upholds constitutional claims only if they were within the specific contemplation of the Framers in effect establishes a presumption of resolving textual ambiguities against the claim of constitutional right. It is far from clear what justifies such a presumption against claims of right. Nothing intrinsic in the nature of interpretation—if there is such a thing as the "nature" of interpretation—commands such a passive approach to ambiguity. This is a choice no less political than any other; it expresses antipathy to claims of the minority to rights against the majority. Those who would restrict claims of right to the values of 1789 specifically articulated in the Constitution turn a blind eye to social progress and eschew adaptation of overarching principles to changes of social circumstance.

Another, perhaps more sophisticated, response to the potential power of judicial interpretation stresses democratic theory: because ours is a government of the people's elected representatives, substantive value choices should by and large be left to them. This view emphasizes not the transcendant historical authority of the framers but the predominant contemporary authority of the elected branches of government. Yet it has similar consequences for the nature of proper judicial interpretation. Faith in the majoritarian process counsels restraint. Even under more expansive formulations of this approach, judicial review is appropriate only to the extent of ensuring that our democratic process functions smoothly. Thus, for example, we would protect freedom of speech merely to ensure that the people are heard by their representatives, rather than as a separate, substantive value. When, by contrast, society tosses up to the Supreme Court a dispute that would require invalidation of a legislature's substantive policy choice, the Court generally would stay its hand because the Constitution was meant as a plan of government and not as an embodiment of fundamental substantive values.

The view that all matters of substantive policy should be resolved through the majoritarian process has appeal under some circumstances, but I think it ultimately will not do. Unabashed enshrinement of majority will would permit the imposition of a social caste system or wholesale confiscation of property so long as a majority of the authorized legislative body, fairly elected, approved. Our Constitution could not abide such a situation. It is the very purpose of a Constitution—and particularly of the Bill of Rights—to declare certain values transcendent, beyond the reach of temporary political majorities. The majoritarian process cannot be expected to rectify claims of minority right that arise as a response to the outcomes of that very majoritarian process. As James Madison put it:

> The prescriptions in favor of liberty ought to be levelled against that quarter where the greatest danger lies, namely, that which possesses the highest prerogative of power. But this is not found in either the Executive or Legislative departments of Government, but in the body of the people, operating by the majority against the minority. (I Annals 437)

Faith in democracy is one thing, blind faith quite another. Those who drafted our Constitution understood the difference. One cannot read the text without admitting that it embodies substantive value choices; it places certain values beyond the power of any legislature. Obvious are the separation of powers; the privilege of the Writ of Habeas Corpus; prohibition of Bills of Attainder and ex post facto laws; prohibition of cruel and unusual punishments; the requirement of just compensation for official taking of property; the prohibition of laws tending to establish religion or enjoining the free exercise of religion; and, since the Civil War, the banishment of slavery and official race discrimination. With respect to at least such principles, we simply have not constituted ourselves as strict utilitarians. While the Constitution may be amended, such amendments require an immense effort by the People as a whole.

To remain faithful to the content of the Constitution, therefore, an approach to interpreting the text must account for the existence of these substantive value choices, and must accept the ambiguity inherent in the effort to apply them to modern circumstances. The Framers discerned fundamental principles through struggles against particular malefactions of the Crown; the struggle shapes the particular contours of the articulated principles. But our acceptance of the fundamental principles has not and should not bind us to those precise, at times anachronistic, contours. Successive generations of Americans have continued to respect these fundamental choices and adopt them as their own guide to evaluating quite different historical practices. Each generation has the choice to overrule or add to the fundamental principles enunciated by the Framers; the Constitution can be amended or it can be ignored. Yet with respect to its fundamental principles, the text has suffered neither fate. Thus, if I may borrow the words of an esteemed predecessor, Justice Robert Jackson, the burden of judicial interpretation is to translate "the majestic generalities of the Bill of Rights, conceived as part of the pattern of liberal government in the eighteenth century, into concrete restraints on officials dealing with the problems of the twentieth century." (Barnette, 319 U. S. at 639)

We current Justices read the Constitution in the only way that we can: as Twentieth Century Americans. We look to the history of the time of framing and to the intervening history of interpretation. But the ultimate question must be, what do the words of the text mean in our time. For the genius of the Constitution rests not in any static meaning it might have had in a world that is dead and gone, but in the adaptability of its great principles to cope with current problems and current needs. What the constitutional fundamentals meant to the wisdom of other times cannot be their measure to the vision of our time. Similarly, what those fundamentals mean for us, our descendants will learn, cannot be the measure to the vision of their time. This realization is not, I assure you, a novel one of my own creation. Permit me to quote from one of the opinions of our Court, *Weems* v. *United States*, 217 U. S. 349, written nearly a century ago:

> Time works changes, brings into existence new conditions and purposes. Therefore, a principle to be vital must be capable of wider application than the mischief which gave it birth. This is peculiarly true of constitutions. They are not ephemeral enactments, designed to meet passing occasions. They are, to use the words of Chief Justice John Marshall, "designed to approach immortality as nearly as human institutions can approach it." The future is their care and provision for events of good and bad tendencies of which no prophesy can be made. In the application of a constitution, therefore, our contemplation cannot be only of what has been, but of what may be.

Interpretation must account for the transformative purpose of the text. Our Constitution was not intended to preserve a preexisting society but to make a new one, to put in place new principles that the prior political community had not sufficiently recognized. Thus, for example, when we interpret the Civil War Amendments to the charter—abolishing slavery, guaranteeing blacks equality under law, and guaranteeing blacks the right to vote—we must remember that those who put them in place had no desire to enshrine the status quo. Their goal was to make over their world, to eliminate all vestige of slave caste.

Having discussed at some length how I, as a Supreme Court Justice, interact with this text, I think it time to turn to the fruits of this discourse. For the Constitution is a sublime oration on the dignity of man, a bold commitment by a people to the ideal of libertarian dignity protected through law. Some reflection is perhaps required before this can be seen.

The Constitution on its face is, in large measure, a structuring text, a blueprint for government. And when the text is not prescribing the form of government it is limiting the powers of that government. The original document, before addition of any of the amendments, does not speak primarily of the rights of man, but of the abilities and disabilities of government. When one reflects upon the text's preoccupation with the scope of government as well as its shape, however, one comes to understand that what this text is about is the relationship of the individual and the state. The text marks the metes and bounds of official authority and individual autonomy. When one studies the boundary that the text marks out, one gets a sense of the vision of the individual embodied in the Constitution.

As augmented by the Bill of Rights and the Civil War Amendments, this text is a sparkling vision of the supremacy of the human dignity of every individual. This vision is reflected in the very choice of democratic self-governance: The supreme value of a democracy is the presumed worth of each individual. And this vision manifests itself most dramatically in the specific prohibitions of the Bill of Rights, a term which I henceforth will apply to describe not only the original first eight amendments, but the Civil War amendments as well. It is a vision that has guided us as a people throughout our history, although the precise rules by which we have protected fundamental human dignity have been transformed over time in response to both transformations of social condition and evolution of our concepts of human dignity.

Until the end of the nineteenth century, freedom and dignity in our country found meaningful protection in the institution of real property. In a society still largely agricultural, a piece of land provided men not just with sustenance but with the means of economic independence, a necessary precondition of political independence and expression. Not surprisingly, property relationships formed the heart of litigation and of legal practice, and lawyers and judges tended to think stable property relationships the highest aim of the law.

But the days when common law property relationships dominated litigation and legal practice are past. To a growing extent economic existence now depends on less certain relationships with government—licenses, employment, contracts, subsidies, unemployment benefits, tax exemptions, welfare and the like. Government participation in the economic existence of individuals is pervasive and deep. Administrative matters and other dealings with government are at the epicenter of the exploding law. We turn to government and to the law for controls which would never have been expected or tolerated before this century, when a man's answer to economic oppression or difficulty was to move two hundred miles west. Now hundreds of thousands of Americans live entire lives without any real prospect of the dignity and autonomy that ownership of real property could confer. Protection of the human dignity of such citizens requires a much modified view of the proper relationship of individual and state.

In general, problems of the relationship of the citizen with government have multiplied and thus have engendered some of the most important constitutional issues of the day. As government acts ever more deeply upon those areas of our lives once marked "private," there is an even greater need to see that individual rights are not curtailed or cheapened in the interest of what may temporarily appear to be the "public good." And as government continues in its role of provider for so many of our disadvantaged citizens, there is an even greater need to ensure that government act with integrity and consistency in its dealings with these citizens. To put this another way, the possibilities for collision between government activity and individual rights will increase as the power and authority of government itself expands, and this growth, in turn, heightens the need for constant vigilance at the collision points. If our free society is to endure, those who govern must recognize human dignity and accept the enforcement of constitutional limitations on their power conceived by the Framers to be necessary to preserve that dignity and the air of freedom which is our proudest heritage. Such recognition will not come from a technical understanding of the organs of government, or the new forms of wealth they administer. It requires something different, something deeper—a personal confrontation with the well-springs of our society. Solutions of constitutional questions from that perspective have become the great challenge of the modern era. All the talk in the last half-decade about shrinking the government does not alter this reality or the challenge it imposes. The modern activist state is a concomitant of the complexity of modern society; it is inevitably with us. We must meet the challenge rather than wish it were not before us.

The challenge is essentially, of course, one to the capacity of our constitutional structure to foster and protect the freedom, the dignity, and the rights of all persons within our borders, which it is the great design of the Constitution to secure. During the time of my public service this challenge has largely taken shape within the confines of the interpretive question whether the specific guarantees of the Bill of Rights operate as restraints on the power of State government. We recognize the Bill of Rights as the primary source of express information as to what is meant by constitutional liberty. The safeguards enshrined in it are deeply etched in the foundation of America's freedoms. Each is a protection with centuries of history behind it, often dearly bought with the blood and lives of people determined to prevent oppression by their rulers. The first eight Amendments, however, were added to the Constitution to operate solely against federal power. It was not until the Thirteenth and Fourteenth Amendments were added, in 1865 and 1868, in response to a demand for national protection against abuses of state power, that the Constitution could be interpreted to require application of the first eight amendments to the states.

It was in particular the Fourteenth Amendment's guarantee that no person be deprived of life, liberty, or property without process of law that led us to apply many of the specific guarantees of the Bill of Rights to the States. In my judgment, Justice Cardozo best captured the reasoning that brought us to such decisions when he described what the Court has done as a process by which the guarantees "have been taken over from the earlier articles of the federal bill of rights and brought within the Fourteenth Amendment by a process of absorption . . . [that] has had its source in the belief that neither liberty nor justice would exist if [those guarantees] . . . were sacrificed." (Palko, 302 U. S., at 326) But this process of absorption was neither swift nor steady. As late as 1922 only the Fifth Amendment guarantee of just compensation for official taking of property had been given force against the states. Between then and 1956 only the First Amendment guarantees of speech and conscience and the Fourth Amendment ban of unreasonable searches and seizures had been incorporated—the latter, however, without the exclusionary rule to give it force. As late as 1961, I could stand before a distinguished assemblage of the bar at New York University's James Madison Lecture and list the following as guarantees that had not been thought to be sufficiently fundamental to the protection of human dignity so as to be enforced against the states: the prohibition of cruel and unusual punishments, the right against self-incrimination, the right to assistance of counsel in a criminal trial, the right to confront witnesses, the right to compulsory process, the right not to be placed in jeopardy of life or limb more than once upon accusation of a crime, the right not to have illegally obtained evidence introduced at a criminal trial, and the right to a jury of one's peers.

The history of the quarter century following that Madison Lecture need not be told in great detail. Suffice it to say that each of the guarantees listed above has been recognized as a fundamental aspect of ordered liberty. Of course, the above catalogue encompasses only the rights of the criminally accused, those caught, rightly or wrongly, in the maw of the criminal justice system. But it has been well said that there is no better test of a society than how it treats those accused of transgressing against it. Indeed, it is because we recognize that incarceration strips a man of his dignity that we demand strict adherence to fair procedure and proof of guilt beyond a reasonable doubt before taking such a drastic step. These requirements are, as Justice Harlan once said, "bottomed on a fundamental value determination of our society that it is far worse to convict an innocent man than to let a guilty man go free." (Winship, 397 U. S., at 372) There is no worse injustice than wrongly to strip a man of his dignity. And our adherence to the constitutional vision of human dignity is so strict that even after convicting a person according to these stringent standards, we demand that his dignity be infringed only to the extent appropriate to the crime and never by means of wanton infliction of pain or deprivation. I interpret the Constitution plainly to embody these fundamental values.

Of course the constitutional vision of human dignity has, in this past quarter century, infused far more than our decisions about the criminal process. Recognition of the principle of "one person, one vote" as a constitutional one redeems the promise of self-governance by affirming the essential dignity of every citizen in the right to equal participation in the democratic process. Recognition of so-called "new property" rights in those receiving government entitlements affirms the essential dignity of the least fortunate among us by demanding that government treat with decency, integrity and consistency those dependent on its benefits for their very survival. After all, a legislative majority initially decides to create governmental entitlements; the Constitution's Due Process Clause merely provides protection for entitlements thought necessary by society as a whole. Such due process rights prohibit government from imposing the devil's bargain of bartering away human dignity in exchange for human sustenance. Likewise, recognition of full equality for women—equal protection of the laws—ensures that gender has no bearing on claims to human dignity.

Recognition of broad and deep rights of expression and of conscience reaffirm the vision of human dignity in many ways.

They too redeem the promise of self-governance by facilitating—indeed demanding—robust, uninhibited, and wide-open debate on issues of public importance. Such public debate is of course vital to the development and dissemination of political ideas. As importantly, robust public discussion is the crucible in which personal political convictions are forged. In our democracy, such discussion is a political duty; it is the essence of self government. The constitutional vision of human dignity rejects the possibility of political orthodoxy imposed from above; it respects the right of each individual to form and to express political judgments, however far they may deviate from the mainstream and however unsettling they might be to the powerful or the elite. Recognition of these rights of expression and conscience also frees up the private space for both intellectual and spiritual development free of government dominance, either blatant or subtle. Justice Brandeis put it so well sixty years ago when he wrote: "Those who won our independence believed that the final end of the State was to make men free to develop their faculties; and that in its government the deliberative forces should prevail over the arbitrary. They valued liberty both as an end and as a means." (Whitney, 274 U. S., at 375)

I do not mean to suggest that we have in the last quarter century achieved a comprehensive definition of the constitutional ideal of human dignity. We are still striving toward that goal, and doubtless it will be an eternal quest. For if the interaction of this Justice and the constitutional text over the years confirms any single proposition, it is that the demands of human dignity will never cease to evolve.

Indeed, I cannot in good conscience refrain from mention of one grave and crucial respect in which we continue, in my judgment, to fall short of the constitutional vision of human dignity. It is in our continued tolerance of State-administered execution as a form of punishment. I make it a practice not to comment on the constitutional issues that come before the Court, but my position on this issue, of course, has been for some time fixed and immutable. I think I can venture some thoughts on this particular subject without transgressing my usual guideline too severely.

As I interpret the Constitution, capital punishment is under all circumstances cruel and unusual punishment prohibited by the Eighth and Fourteenth Amendments. This is a position of which I imagine you are not unaware. Much discussion of the merits of capital punishment has in recent years focused on the potential arbitrariness that attends its administration, and I have no doubt that such arbitrariness is a grave wrong. But for me, the wrong of capital punishment transcends such procedural issues. As I have said in my opinions, I view the Eighth Amendment's prohibition of cruel and unusual punishments as embodying to a unique degree moral principles that substantively restrain the punishments our civilized society may impose on those persons who transgress its laws. Foremost among the moral principles recognized in our cases and inherent in the prohibition is the primary principle that the State, even as it punishes, must treat its citizens in a manner consistent with their intrinsic worth as human beings. A punishment must not be so severe as to be utterly and irreversibly degrading to the very essence of human dignity. Death for whatever crime and under all circumstances is a truly awesome punishment. The calculated killing of a human being by the State involves, by its very nature, an absolute denial of the executed person's humanity. The most vile murder does not, in my view, release the State from constitutional restraints on the destruction of human dignity. Yet an executed person has lost the very right to have rights, now or ever. For me, then, the fatal constitutional infirmity of capital punishment is that it treats members of the human race as nonhumans, as objects to be toyed with and discarded. It is, indeed, "cruel and unusual." It is thus inconsistent with the fundamental premise of the Clause that even the most base criminal remains a human being possessed of some potential, at least, for common human dignity.

This is an interpretation to which a majority of my fellow Justices—not to mention, it would seem, a majority of my fellow countrymen—does not subscribe. Perhaps you find my adherence to it, and my recurrent publication of it, simply contrary, tiresome, or quixotic. Or perhaps you see in it a refusal to abide by the judicial principle of *stare decisis*, obedience to precedent. In my judgment, however, the unique interpretive role of the Supreme Court with respect to the Constitution demands some flexibility with respect to the call of *stare decisis*. Because we are the last word on the meaning of the Constitution, our views must be subject to revision over time, or the Constitution falls captive, again, to the anachronistic views of long-gone generations. I mentioned earlier the judge's role in seeking out the community's interpretation of the Constitutional text. Yet, again in my judgment, when a Justice perceives an interpretation of the text to have departed so far from its essential meaning, that Justice is bound, by a larger constitutional duty to the community, to expose the departure and point toward a different path. On this issue, the death penalty, I hope to embody a community striving for human dignity for all, although perhaps not yet arrived.

You have doubtless observed that this description of my personal encounter with the constitutional text has in large portion been a discussion of public developments in constitutional doctrine over the last quarter century. That, as I suggested at the outset, is inevitable because my interpretive career has demanded a public reading of the text. This public encounter with the text, however, has been a profound source of personal inspiration. The vision of human dignity embodied there is deeply moving. It is timeless. It has inspired Americans for two centuries and it will continue to inspire as it continues to evolve. That evolutionary process is inevitable and, indeed, it is the true interpretive genius of the text.

If we are to be as a shining city upon a hill, it will be because of our ceaseless pursuit of the constitutional ideal of human dignity. For the political and legal ideals that form the foundation of much that is best in American institutions— ideals jealously preserved and guarded throughout our history—still form the vital force in creative political thought and activity within the nation today. As we adapt our institutions to the ever-changing conditions of national and international life, those ideals of human dignity—liberty and justice for all individuals—will continue to inspire and guide us because they are entrenched in our Constitution. The Constitution with its Bill of Rights thus has a bright future, as well as a glorious past, for its spirit is inherent in the aspirations of our people.

ACADEMIC FREEDOM OR LICENSE?

ACADEMIC FREEDOM OR ACADEMIC LICENSE?[1]

LASZLO CSORBA III[2]

In April 1985, a new non-profit corporation, Accuracy in Academia, was established. Its president, Malcolm Lawrence, stated its purpose in a speech at Iowa State University on September 25, 1985, as follows:

> The corporation is formed for the purpose of educating the public, the learned societies, professional educators, and academicians as to desirable standards of accuracy and truth in academia with respect to objective truth and fairness. In furtherance of these objectives, the corporation shall examine cases in which academic performance is alleged to fall short of these standards and it shall publicize its findings. The corporation shall publish and distribute literature, provide speakers at seminars and other meetings and gatherings, conduct classes, cooperate with other like-minded societies and corporations and individuals, and employ such other means as are deemed feasible by the Board of Directors to communicate to the public its views on the standards of accuracy and truth in academia.

Accuracy in Academia is a spin-off of Accuracy in Media (AIM), an organization founded 16 years earlier to monitor the news media—newspapers, radio, and television. Accuracy in Academia grew out of the belief of Reed Irvine, founder of AIM, that journalistic reports were out of line with the thinking of the majority of Americans, and that the explanation for this was "related to the fact that most journalists today are the products of our liberal arts colleges, where our youth are being indoctrinated with views and values radically different from those of mainstream America" ("Why Accuracy in Academia," published by Accuracy in Academia). AIA President Malcolm Lawrence claimed that 10,000 known Marxists teach on university campuses (Keith B. Richburg, *Washington Post*, August 4, 1984, p. A7). To ferret out those professors who they believe are instilling a leftist bias in young minds, AIA organized a program to recruit student volunteers to identify suspected leftists, audit their courses, and challenge them publicly, if necessary. They also began publication of *Campus Report*, a monthly newsletter in which they report on individuals accused of trying to indoctrinate students with inaccurate or "un-American" ideas.

The formation of Accuracy in Academia sparked a sharp response from many academics and civil libertarians, who viewed it as the latest in

[1]Delivered as part of the William James Forum Lecture Series in Hyson Lounge of Hodson Hall, Washington College, Chestertown, Maryland, at 7:30 P.M. on February 5, 1986.

[2]For biographical note, see Appendix.

a series of New Right assaults on academic freedom and the open exchange of ideas. For others it evoked memories of Joe McCarthy and campus witch-hunts.

In a speech delivered at Washington College on February 5, 1986, Laszlo Csorba III, the 22-year-old executive director of Accuracy in Academia, explained the purpose of the organization and sought to convince his audience of its worth. An address by Chancellor Joseph S. Murphy of the City University offering a different perspective follows Csorba's speech (see p. 101).

Csorba was invited to address Washington College students, faculty members, and other interested persons as part of the William James Forum, which for more than 25 years has presented about one lecture a month during the school year by controversial and/or political speakers to the small (750 students) but distinguished liberal arts campus in Chestertown, Maryland. The Forum, which has no partisan basis, seeks to present speakers of differing viewpoints on a wide variety of issues.

Csorba presented his speech to 100 to 125 students, faculty members, and Chestertown community members (a large turnout for the small school). In a letter to the editor of this volume, Professor Peter Tapke, Adviser to the Forum, reported:

> Mr. Csorba's talk was followed by a lively question period. As would be expected, he was questioned rather vigorously by the sizeable number of faculty members present, and by students as well. In my judgment he replied to these questions directly, and with courtesy, poise, and effectiveness. This very bright young man is clearly on top of the facts in the issues he is dealing with, and is an impressive public speaker. At the close of the program he was warmly applauded. (Letter of May 2, 1986)

However, the college's news bureau observed, "His reception was less than warm. There were a few heated words exchanged."

The day after Csorba's talk, the college student newspaper carried an interview with the speaker and an editorial which commended the William James Forum for bringing Csorba to the campus, but warned that AIA "is a form of intimidation . . . [which] must not be allowed to turn into an ideological witchhunt." The editorial maintained:

> It is the students, faculty peers, and college administrators, not some outside politically biased organization, who have the right and responsibility to determine a faculty member's status. (Chestertown, Maryland, *Washington College Elm*, February 7, 1986, p. 2)

Laszlo Csorba III's speech: I would like to thank Dr. Peter Tapke and Washington College for inviting me here tonight to express my thoughts on a subject of great importance to college students and professors in America—academic freedom.

I would also like to thank you all for your hospitality, the nice reception, and a fine meal. I always enjoy getting away from Washington D.C., even only if it's for a few hours. I can tell you, with all the criticism my organization has received and some of the political wars that go on in that town, it's hard to find many friends in Washington, D.C. President Truman once said, "If you want a friend in Washington, buy a dog."

Let me say that I was honored to receive your invitation and noticed that I am among many noted figures who have participated in your forum. As such, I felt compelled to write a speech and offer it to you formally for your pleasure or disgust.

I would like to speak to you tonight about the issue of academic freedom, its function, its proper use, and its definition, and how it occasionally is abused—what we might call academic license. Before I get to that, let me offer my own testimony as one who has ventured recently to criticize the men and women of academy.

Since Reed Irvine founded Accuracy in Academia to publicize cases of academic inaccuracy, political imbalances, examples of intolerance, and incidents of indoctrination, there has been an uproar in academia not heard since William F. Buckley wrote his book, *God and Man at Yale, the Superstitions of Academic Freedom*. Before Accuracy in Academia even got its first publication off, we heard all the usual cries, and threats and denunciations. "McCarthyism," "fascism," "censorship," and our old friend the "chilling effect" all made their expected appearances. Now the first rule in scholarship, as I understand it, is to gather up your facts. And this rule applies in most every other profession as well. But what of these scholarly critics—where were their facts? On what were they basing their criticism? Had they waited a few weeks, they might have had the opportunity to read over the newsletter. Surely that would have been the more scholarly approach.

Now the simple truth of the matter is this. Our organization was founded to encourage debate in classroom, not to stifle or restrain it. Just consider what we are doing at this very moment. I have raised an idea—that teaching is not indoctrinating—and here we are discussing it. And the only people who object to our doing so are the professors who most fear public criticism.

Instead of dealing with our questions in serious debate, they would rather do battle with the caricature—with the jack-booted brownshirts they see running up and down the halls, crashing down lecturns and hauling innocent scholars like themselves out for interrogation. They have as many illusions about their critics as they do about themselves.

As Hoover Institution Fellow Thomas Sowell wrote in a recent nationally syndicated column, "Parents, students, taxpayers have a right to know what's going on. Accuracy in Academia has no power to do anything more than tell them." He concluded by writing, "Deep thinkers are worried about the confrontation—not about the cancerous problem that requires it."

Think about it for a moment. This organization has been denounced by hundreds of professors, nine major academic organizations, and hundreds of journalists. And besides being covered by almost every major publication in the U.S.A., we have been attacked in a recent Doonesbury cartoon by Garry Trudeau and have been condemned by the Soviet Union three times, on three consecutive front pages of *Izvestia*, the main daily in Moscow.

Izvestia's story said, "Teachers at universities are quivering with fear. They tremble at the utterance of each word." A professor at Chico State University wrote, "The existence of AIA is in the back of your mind. It's like AIDS—you know it exists, so you're cautious of it."

However, there have been some calm, well-reasoned replies to this organization—an organization which only has two full-time staffmembers working out of one office.

Boston University President John Silber recently said on the CBS Nightwatch program—which was then later quoted in the *Wall Street Journal* and other newspapers around the country—that " . . . I don't think that anything serious is going to happen to the professors beyond the fact that it may become a matter of broad public knowledge that they don't know what they're talking about. Now if a professor can't stand the simple exposure of his ignorance to the general public, he should get into a different line of work."

Silber added that teaching is a form of publication and professors cannot claim immunity from public criticism.

Just a few weeks ago on "This Week with David Brinkley," it was columnist George Will, a former professor himself, who strongly defended AIA. He said, "The professors seem to be saying that a lecturer and his students have a kind of priestly relationship in a confessional, that it's private. It's oral publication and it ought to be talked about."

In response to Hodding Carter's claim that AIA might threaten the professor's tenure, Will responded, "But if Accuracy in Academia identifies some professor as left-wing, they'll buy him a round of drinks at the faculty club. He won't get fired. They'll wash his Volvo for him."

Nonetheless, some say that reporting on professors in the classroom threatens "academic freedom." Some others say, like the *New York Times*, that students sending reports about their professors to a national newspaper will cause a chilling effect, and ultimately academic freedom will be in danger. I agree, academic freedom is indeed threatened on the campuses of America, but for other more obvious reasons—reasons that I hope to document by discussing this notion of academic freedom, how it should be applied, and the responsibilities that professors have in conjunction with this ambiguous right.

Firstly, academic freedom is simply not the right of free speech. We give this particular freedom the name "academic freedom" to denote its academic function. The first word qualifies the second. It only confuses the issue, then, to invoke the right of free speech—or "freedom of conscience," or "intellectual freedom." These are personal liberties which we all enjoy and they are not in question. But, academic freedom, by definition, is a professional right that one exercises only in the course of carrying out certain professional responsibilities.

We must ask ourselves whether professors are defending a scholarly right, or protecting ideological privileges—academic freedom or academic license?

Last February the prestigious Association of American Colleges published a report entitled "Integrity in the College Curriculum" which gives an understanding to some of the responsibilities of professors. The report states that "The corporate responsibility of the faculty for the curriculum as a whole extends to responsibility for forceful defense of academic freedom. In their special responsibilities to students, college and university teachers are required, however, not to use the classroom as a platform for propagandizing. Professional ethics demand that they be balanced and that they be fair. Instruction is an instrument of inquiry, not indoctrination. Inquiry requires freedom, indoctrination stifles it."

Now here comes the part of this report where I would add special emphasis. It reads,

> Professors, by virtue of their responsibilities and privileges in learned positions of great public trust, must place the interests, welfare, and legitimate rights of students above all other considerations; that is what constitutes a professional relationship.

Now if we were to judge by the number of times we hear the phrase "academic freedom" used, then we would have to assume that the right of academic freedom flourishes not only here, but all across the land. At colleges everywhere professors speak of their "academic freedom." Unfortunately, we all know what talk is worth. To speak reverently of a right is one thing, to practise that right responsibly and extend it to others is something a little different, something a little more difficult. And to see whether this right flourishes, we have to consider how it is practised, never mind how often we hear the phrase spoken, or how passionately.

The University Professors for Academic Order, which has members such as Milton Friedman, Russell Kirk, various congressmen and senators, and a dozen college presidents—and which incidentally has endorsed Accuracy in Academia—provides for us a definition of academic freedom that seems to illustrate the point that I am attempting to make. It follows that "the University professor, because he has mastered his subject, is entitled to responsible liberty in the presentation of the subject he teaches. However, it is improper for the professor to deliberately intrude material designed to politicize the students, particularly where that material has no direct relation to the subject he is teaching; nor has he a right to fail to present his course as officially announced."

William F. Buckley, who launched his celebrated career by confronting the issue of academic freedom, also provides a well-reasoned definition of academic freedom, that freedom being to investigate and study whatever phenomenon the investigator regards as important. However, such freedom does not mean that the teacher should air whatever opinion he or she prefers within the confines of the classroom without having the empirical documentation to support his scholarly assertions. Once again, responsibility is the key.

Now, I am going to assume that most academics here would recognize the responsibilities which accompany this right of academic freedom. But I know what many scholars will claim. The claim has been made that there is simply no evidence that professors are violating these professional ethics by propagandizing or misinforming their students on a scale as to warrant a national newspaper to publicize these incidents. Let's just take a few concrete examples that come to mind, lest we be too abstract in our discussion of the issue.

To start, let's look locally at a case at the University of Maryland where a professor paused recently in his Humor in American Literature class to make the scholarly observation that there is "more injustice in the United States today than there was in Nazi Germany," basing this comparison on the "sexism, racism, and bigotry" in recent American history.

Or how about the professor at Texas A&M who proclaimed in the daily campus newspaper that "if a student comes into my class and leaves four years later with the same attitudes and beliefs that he came in with, then I have failed." This professor then goes on to say that "I do not believe in the institution of marriage. I am an atheist, and I do not claim any political party. I am not patriotic toward Texas A&M, the flag, or America."

There is the professor at Northwestern University who claims that there was no Holocaust in Hitler's Germany. And then there is the professor in Southern California who claims that somehow blacks are inferior because of the size of their cranium.

In our first publication, we covered a story dealing with a professor at Arizona State University who passed his days in class teaching about all the dangers and horrors of nuclear power. Now whatever you think of this man's cause, the point is that he was advancing that cause day in and day out, in a class entitled "Political Ideologies 101." Surely we can all agree, whatever our political faith or creed, that if you are going to call a course "political ideologies," then it ought to be about political ideologies. That's not a political proposition, but it seems to me, a point of common sense.

This same professor has a book which he assigns to his class each year. It's called *Atom's Eve: Ending the Nuclear Age*, and I highly recommend it as an example of this new brand of scholarship we are talking about.

Midway through this book you hit upon a chronology of the rise and spread of the nuclear age. The major events, good and bad, are all listed in sad succession for 39 pages—everything from Hiroshima to the founding of the Clamshall Alliance. But some events were deemed unsuitable; for example the Baruch Plan, advanced in 1946 to place the development of atomic technology under international supervision. Along with omissions of Soviet treaty violations, this bit of American history was apparently of no relevance—unlike the Clamshall Alliance.

And then there are the Marxist academics, committed, as *U.S. News and World Report* put it, to undermining the American capitalistic system in the classrooms of America. Saul Landau, a visiting Marxist lecturer to my former college, the University of California, Davis, required students to attend all of his propaganda films for Cuban communism, including the movie "Fidel" which shows the warm-hearted dictator playing baseball, visiting his nursery school, and driving through the Cuban countryside.

No mention of the human rights violations in that country, including the torturing of political prisoners, the absence of a free press, free speech, and free elections. Landau went as far as to say to a campus reporter that Castro is not a dictator. But what can be expected of a man who wrote in 1976 to a friend in Cuba that he was now "dedicated to making propaganda for American socialism."

And then there is New York University Marxist Professor Bertell Ollman, who was even more candid about his goals when he wrote that the task of Marxist professors in America is "make more revolutionaries . . . the revolution will only come when there are enough of us to make it."

And most recently *The Campus Report*'s headline story was about a Princeton professor who admitted to serious factual errors in his book *The Collapse of the Weimar Republic*. To buttress his argument that Hitler collaborated closely with German industrialists, this professor simply invented quotations and altered documentary evidence. In fact, out of 70 footnotes that were checked by another professor reading the book, only 4 were actually correct. But he is now a hero among radical historians because his book happens to confirm their Marxist theories.

It is simply amusing to see how far these professors will go in trying to find fault with the United States and its highly successful free market system. Nobel Laureate George Wald of Harvard, for example, thought that he found a serious flaw in the free market system. He said that poor people in this country were suffering from diseases because iodized salt cost more than non-iodized salt and they couldn't afford to buy it. When Dr. Thomas Jukes of U.C. Berkeley pointed out to him that the cost of iodizing salt was minuscule and that the salt companies charge the same price for both the iodized and non-iodized product, Dr. Wald lapsed into silence.

In correcting George Wald's misinformation about the price of salt, Dr. Jukes was reminding this famous scientist that he should derive his theories from facts, not *vice versa.*

And then there are the hundreds of cases of intolerance on the campuses today regarding university guest lecturers and professors who are harassed, not allowed to speak, and even fired from their positions. You have all heard about the cases of Jeane Kirkpatrick, Casper Weinberger, and Henry Kissinger attempting to speak on the campuses, but being disallowed by a militant minority. Recently, *The Campus Report* covered the case where Aldofo Calero, commander of the Nicaraguan Democratic Resistance, traveled to Northwestern University, but was unable to speak after faculty members and students continuously disrupted him and then threw fresh blood on him.

And in our first *Campus Report* we covered the case of Fordham University professor Phyllis Zagano who was fired from her position apparently because she held strong traditional Catholic views.

Finally, we heard from students at Oakland University in Michigan that their history professor had made the case that the Sandinistas have not committed human rights violations against the Mosquito Indians since 1979 and 1980, a point even refuted by some of the Reagan Administration's strongest critics in Congress. I can go on and on and on. But I think the point is clear enough. Before Accuracy in Academia came along, many of these deceptions, examples of intolerance and attempts to indoctrinate, were never brought to the attention of those who support these academics.

Yes, right away let us all say, that these professors have a right to their views. That right is not in question. The question is simply whether apart from all the rights and privileges these professors enjoy, there are not a few responsibilities that come with the vocation. We all know what their rights are; what we need to clarify, I think, are their responsibilities.

I suppose the best way to put my position is that academic freedom serves an academic purpose, and not an ideological one. Teachers enjoy this right so that they can teach. And if they are not using it for that purpose, then the right simply does not apply. Yes, a professor is just as entitled as the rest of us to engage in political activism. But he's not entitled to call it scholarship. And neither, I'm sorry to say, is he immune from public criticism once he has decided to mix those two vocations. He can't vent his grievances in the classroom, and then insulate himself against any criticism that returns his way.

The issue is not whether any of these academic visionaries have a right to believe in whatever they please. I know that's redundant; but I must emphasize this again. The question is whether in advancing their doctrines they are engaging in scholarship or ideological polemics. The proposition, "I have a right to profess my opinions," does not lead logically to "and you must hire me to do so."

So the next question becomes what are the limits to academic freedom, if it has any limits at all? And the only way to determine the limits of any right is to ask yourself what its purpose is. Why are teachers granted this right?

Surely, it was not for their own benefit alone. Universities were not set up around the country merely to provide malcontents with a means of registering their grievances against society. There are others involved here; their students, for instance. Some of these people have got the idea that academic freedom is simply a means we use to protect and nurture such valuable national assets as themselves. And indeed, they can be an asset, but only in so far as they perform the service of education.

Professors, however, have argued that "we are teaching as we see fit. Our subjects have to do with values, which after all are subjective. We give our interpretation, and that's all we can do."

This is not only a sophism, but an admission of professional incompetence. If it's all a matter of interpretation, why then we are all equally qualified to teach a college course. The argument destroys its own credentials. Think about it. Yes, of course a professor will inevitably have his own opinions, and of course some things can be taught only by one's own interpretation. But his mere opinions are presumably not what got him the job in the first place, or what qualifies him to keep his position.

There must be something more—some concrete knowledge of his subject or discipline which makes him an expert worth listening to, and not just another man with an opinion, sounding off like the rest of us. There must be something which confers a particular dignity on the vocation.

And what might that be? A narrow but useful formulation might be this: Whatever it is that a scholar and a college professor is uniquely suited to do—*that* is what he ought to be doing. And given the demands of those tasks, very little else.

I submit to you tonight, in conclusion, that academic freedom is a vital right on the college campuses, and indeed it is threatened. But the worst threat to any right is the man who abuses it.

In seven short months since this organization has existed, I have witnessed the abuses of academic freedom in the hundreds of letters from students and professors from all across the country that have crossed my desk. But if I were to give you a final appraisal of the current understanding of academic freedom and whether it flourishes in academia today, sadly I would have to say that academic freedom is nothing more than a useful device which gives license to some people, and silences others.

ACCURACY IN ACADEMIA[1]

JOSEPH S. MURPHY[2]

In an article entitled "Campus Conservatives on the Offensive" *U. S. News and World Report* noted on January 13, 1986, that

> On campuses across the country, the political right is adopting tactics used for years by liberal students protesting racial segregation and the Vietnam War. Encouraged by President Reagan's popularity and concerned over their economic future, young conservatives are speaking out where they once hesitated on issues ranging from military power to Marxism (p. 20).

"Perhaps the most controversial political development on campuses," according to the magazine, "is the furor triggered by a Washington-based group called Accuracy in Academia." Formed for the avowed purpose of challenging liberal professors who it says feed biased information to students, AIA claimed to have more than 200 anonymous student volunteers monitoring and reporting on classroom lectures around the country at the end of 1985 (*Time*, December 23, 1985, p. 57). (For additional information on the group and its goals, see pp. 91–92.)

Accuracy in Academia was the target of a speech delivered by Dr. Joseph S. Murphy, Chancellor of the City University of New York, to a convocation on "Current Threats to Academic Freedom" on November 14, 1985. Spurred by the emergence of new challenges to academic freedom, the American Association of University Professors [AAUP] sponsored the day-long convocation, which included representatives of 37 of the endorsing organizations of the 1940 *Statement of Principles on Academic Free-*

[1]Delivered to a convocation on "Current Threats to Academic Freedom" sponsored by the American Association of University Professors at 10 A.M., November 14, 1985, at the Washington Plaza Hotel, Washington, D.C.

[2]For biographical note, see Appendix.

dom and Tenure, as well as visitors from a wide variety of higher education associations, colleges and universities, and the media.

Following welcoming remarks by the president of the AAUP and the president of the Association of American Colleges, Chancellor Murphy delivered the first speech at a session devoted to "Accuracy in Academia," one of six topics covered in the course of the meeting.

Murphy began his address with a blunt statement:

> Let me begin by putting the subject of Accuracy in Academia in some perspective. Unlike some of my colleagues, I do not view this group, in and of itself, as a major threat to the idea or the practice of academic freedom. It may become that in due time; the forces that it represents certainly pose as grave a menace to the free exchange of ideas in our society as they do to the existence and extension of economic and political freedom. As of November 1985, however, the Accuracy in Academia organization, with its budget of $50,000 and its full-time professional staff of one, represents only an irritation.

However, Murphy went on to denounce the long-range threat of such organizations in what *Time* called "an impassioned address" in which he "blasted" the group for recruiting students "as a corps of thought police" (December 23, 1985, p. 57).

The media gave Chancellor Murphy's speech, attended by about 150 people, wide coverage. Leading newspapers such as the *New York Times*, the *Washington Post*, and the *Christian Science Monitor* carried detailed reports on it and later published editorial reactions. The Associated Press and the major news magazines also covered the speech.

Joseph S. Murphy's speech: Let me begin by putting the subject of Accuracy in Academia in some perspective.

Unlike some of my colleagues, I do not view this group, in and of itself, as a major threat to the idea or the practice of academic freedom. It may become that in due time; the forces that it represents certainly pose as grave a menace to the free exchange of ideas in our society as they do to the existence and extension of economic and political freedom. As of November 1985, however, the Accuracy in Academia organization, with its budget of $50,000 and its full-time professional staff of one, represents only an irritation.

It may be, ironically, a useful irritation. Like most of the other fringe entities with which we have become familiar in recent years, this group combines a paucity of valid ideas with an impressive capacity for media manipulation. It has already pushed itself and its concerns onto a dozen television talk shows, the pages of a hundred newspapers, the American consciousness, and the agenda of the AAUP [American Association of University

Professors]. In doing so it has given us the opportunity to restate the case for academic freedom—what Einstein called "the right to search for the truth and to publish and teach what one holds to be true."

The arguments on our side of the issue can be stated in simple terms.

Why is free expression of ideas, whether in the classroom or the pages of a journal or, for that matter, on a street corner, a right of moral value? Not solely because it represents a fundamental tenet of our national tradition, embedded in the Constitution and in a two-century-old body of case law; private property rights, after all, have a similar constitutional and case law basis and few among us hold those to be sacred. We contend that there is something of greater import about academic freedom that impels us to defend it from attack from whatever quarter.

To put it directly, we believe in the proliferation of ideas. We believe especially in the promulgation of ideas that put to the test the dominant hypotheses and the dominant class and social structures of our culture—ideas that challenge economic and political hegemony. We believe this not because we are revolutionaries or Marxists, by and large: Even Accuracy in Academia admits that ninety-eight percent of us in the profession are not. Our reason for defending what some would call the right to subversive thought is more profound. We believe that when the dominant ideology is subjected to the test of competing ideas it will emerge stronger, more resilient, more valid than before, or it will be transformed by the intellectual force of contrary dogma. Either way, society is well served.

We have all seen the process work, at some time or another. Students faced with ideas that run counter to the mainstream notions they brought with them to college—generally the middle-class world view inculcated by the media and the elementary and secondary school system—test and modify those notions, or cling to them more tightly than before, more confident of their truth. Defenders of the prevailing ways of thought and action in the larger community will, when confronted with a dissident perspective, refine their arguments and develop new proofs. This, at least, is what we aim for—even knowing that it may be a vain hope for the vast majority of students, who are drawn to the university in pursuit of greater earning power. But for a few, the concepts of skeptical thought that guided Galileo and Newton, Darwin and Freud, Marx and Keynes may be a living reality.

The systemic, almost automatic impediments to this kind of freedom are known to most of us. We have, in fact, accepted many of them as basic and immutable facts of our professional lives.

The most important, of course, is our system of tenure tracking and peer review. Tenure exists primarily to protect academic freedom. But let me pose the question: Is there anyone in the profession who has not felt the subtle pressures, in the five years before the awarding of tenure, to stay within a respectable range on the ideological spectrum—and to avoid offensive language and potentially offensive themes, to cover safe issues in preference to inflammatory ones, to use conventional texts instead of those that convey deviant concepts? Some of us rise above the pressure and others do not; all of us feel it. And while, for many, the coercive force stops with the awarding of tenure or the final promotion to full professor, for the rest it becomes so internalized that they become in the end the defenders (or the enforcers) of conformity.

But there are other threats as well. In recent days we have seen this Administration announce its plans to use federal funds—Star Wars funds—to lure faculty into personally lucrative research efforts. They promise that technology developed with public sector defense grants can then be peddled for individual gain in private sector markets. Coercion can come in many forms, and we may soon have evidence on this issue that grants can be as inimical to free thought as is out and out censorship.

The drive to turn universities into tools of economic productivity, with the encouragement of more contractual linkages between the campus and the corporation, poses another set of threats; how many institutions will jeopardize big dollars for the sake of a few faculty members lingering loudly outside the dominant consensus and criticizing capitalism in general and the affiliated corporations in particular? As colleges compete for more private sector dollars, how many will be immune from the fear that a negative press created by dissident professors will alienate potential clients, as it might alienate potential students and potential donors?

These are serious concerns, but they move us away from the topic of the moment, Accuracy in Academia.

What we have before us, in my view, is a group that exists largely as a symptom of serious underlying problems: the frustrated national quest for simplistic philosophical truth in a confusing time, mirrored in the same quest that accounts for much of Ronald Reagan's mandate. It has spawned an anti-intellectualism characteristic of an era in which our leaders give us at best a vacuous ideology such as in the 1950's and the 1920's, and an expression of anger at large and powerful institutions wrongly perceived to be antithetical to the goals of those people who define themselves as part of the American middle class.

It may be beyond our present capacity to address those larger concerns. We can, at least, address Accuracy in Academia, and do so in a way that will win those outside of the profession to our cause.

For over two hundred years this society has tolerated the existence of reactionary forces who include the academy prominently among their targets of attack. In this sense Accuracy in Academia is only the latest chorus of an old song. We have coexisted with such groups in the past; why not simply shrug this one off now?

For two reasons:

First and most obvious is Accuracy in Academia's totally offensive methodology: the recruitment of students (and others incited to enroll as auditors) as a corps of thought-police, the development of a private bureau of investigation, the exposure of private individuals to public condemnation, the announcement and promulgation of some self-defined concept of acceptable truth.

All of us in the profession are repulsed by that means of operation (or ought to be) no less than if the perpetrators of the acts were government agents rather than privately funded vigilantes. Censorship does violence to most of what is good about the American political tradition and all that is worthy in the traditions of the academy. It matters little in the end whether the censors are cloaked in public or private garb.

I cannot speak for the leaders of other institutions. Speaking for myself I can make clear at every opportunity that no group functioning in the manner of Accuracy in Academia will have any influence over any hiring, firing, promotion, or tenure decision, or any other decision, at the City University of New York as long as I am Chancellor.

Second, there is the possibility that this group and those behind it will establish themselves as a significant presence in the public agencies that regulate, fund, and in better times serve as advocates for the higher education community. This has been the case in a host of areas already. It takes no great flight of fantasy to imagine that an Administration that turned to Anne Burford for environmental advice would turn to Reed Irvine and the twenty-two-year-old executive director of Accuracy in Academia for advice about what grants to award and what institutions to help.

How should we in the profession deal with this potential menace? My own approach has several basic elements.

One is a restatement of the essential legitimacy of intellectual freedom, and a clear and cogent denunciation of attempts from any source to restrict it. Such attempts are more than arrogant; they do violence to the fundamental tenets of democratic government.

Secondly, we should present to those members of the public who follow these issues the contention, clear to most of us in the profession, that the very concept of "accuracy" in academia is seductively misleading. Truth is a goal to be pursued rather than a commodity to be packaged. In this society more than in most others, contradiction is an inherent element of ideology and multiple ideologies usually cohabit the same academic space. We cannot identify what is true. At best, we can more or less determine what is the conventional wisdom, what represents a dissident view, and what is outrageously dissident. Apparently what Accuracy in Academia is trying to do is ferret out of higher education all that is outrageous and most of what is dissident. They delude the public, and probably themselves, when they contend that what they are up to has anything to do with truth, or even that they know what it is. On all the important questions, no one does.

Third, we should maintain and extend free access to our campuses to all who come in an orderly manner, whatever their purpose. When Adlai Stevenson was spat upon in Dallas a month before the Kennedy assassination, he was asked if he would send the people who did it to jail. No, he said, he would send them to school. That should be our attitude.

Fourth, we should defend without apology and without concession those cited by any external group as perpetrators of incorrect thought. We may give them the resources they need to respond, but make it clear that from the institution's point of view no response is necessary.

Finally, we should avoid the guilt mentality that has taken root in our profession as it has in most others, the reflexive response to external criticisms that we and we alone can and will remedy any defects extant in our institutions.

The argument, or, if one insists, the concession, that we make should follow a different path. There are indeed defects within the academy, and "inaccuracies" may be among them. Many are simply not susceptible to remediation; they come with the territory. Those who would purge higher education of error would transform higher education into something it should not be—something of trivial value at best, and something of no greater purpose than the advancement of vocationalism. Let us concede the existence of what Accuracy in Academia characterizes as deficiencies, but make the case that they are part and parcel of a valuable whole.

We in the academy are privileged, as are few others in American society, to perform important work to deal with profound ideas, and to examine and explicate the critical issues of our time. But these privileges do not come free. They carry with them profound obligations.

REAFFIRMING THE PAST

ABRAHAM LINCOLN AND OUR "UNFINISHED BUSINESS"[1]

MARIO M. CUOMO[2]

In the months following the stunning success of his keynote address at the 1984 Democratic National Convention (see *Representative American Speeches, 1984–85*, p. 22), Governor Mario M. Cuomo of New York became one of the most sought-after speakers in the country. He also was increasingly mentioned as a potential presidential nominee. Denying that he was a contender, Cuomo nevertheless appeared to many to be seeking the highest office in the land. His choice of speaking engagements from the many invitations extended seemed to lend credence to speculation that he was a candidate.

Whatever Cuomo's intentions, the invitation to address the Abraham Lincoln Association's annual dinner on Lincoln's birthday in Lincoln's home town of Springfield, Illinois, afforded the New Yorker an almost unrivalled forum to present his ideas and philosophy to the American people. The Lincoln Association speech is a tradition begun in 1909, when William Jennings Bryan gave the first address. Since then speakers have included Booker T. Washington, President William Howard Taft, Henry Cabot Lodge, Adlai E. Stevenson, Nelson Rockefeller, Allan Nevins, Willy Brandt, and poet Carl Sandburg.

The event, sponsored by the Lincoln Association and the Illinois State Historical Society, was bipartisan and intended to be non-political. The day's activities included the premiere of a public television documentary, "Mr. Lincoln and Illinois," and a symposium at which history scholars presented papers in the Old State Capitol. Cuomo delivered his address to 600 members of the Abraham Lincoln Association and to political leaders of both parties, plus nearly 100 media representatives. Attendance was almost double that of the previous year; the increase was attributed to Cuomo's appearance.

Accompanied by an honor guard and a marching band that played "When Johnny Comes Marching Home Again," Cuomo was led to the dais through the crowd. He was introduced by Governor James R. Thompson, a Republican, who drew laughter from the predominantly Republican audience by declaring, tongue-in-cheek, "This evening is not about presidential politics." Cuomo returned the political jab, saying, "I wouldn't be a bit surprised—if the election goes well this year for him—if early next year you heard a declaration of interest from a reelected governor of a large state—Jim Thompson."

[1]Delivered to the annual dinner of the Abraham Lincoln Association commemorating Lincoln's birthday, on the evening of February 12, 1986, in the banquet room of the Holiday Inn East, Springfield, Illinois.

[2]For biographical note, see Appendix.

Cuomo, who is known to take a careful and personal interest in the preparation of his speeches, was said to have been "remarkably serious" about preparing the address and to have spent hours with Lincoln scholars and reading about Lincoln. The previous week he had gone on "retreat" to read and write in preparation of the speech (Marc Humbert, Yonkers, New York *Herald Statesman*, February 9, 1986).

Most reporters noted that Cuomo praised Lincoln in his address and used the Republican president's words to bolster his own political philosophies. One journalist observed, "Cuomo delivered one of his signature speeches on the role of government and, in the process, criticized President Reagan without naming him" (Albany *Times Union*, February 13, 1986).

Reaction to the speech, even among Republicans, was generally positive. Reporter Jeannie H. Cross wrote, "Despite a lingering touch of laryngitis, Cuomo was in top form in both jocularity and seriousness as he spoke at the Lincoln Day dinner. . . . Cuomo got rave reviews from virtually everyone." Democratic Senator Paul Simon said, "I was most impressed. It was scholarly, it was sensitive, and yet it had a sense of direction" (John Dowling, Associated Press, February 13, 1986). Republican Governor James R. Thompson of Illinois pronounced it "a great speech—very eloquent. Illinois Democrats were particularly enthusiastic." "He's the most eloquent politician I've ever heard," observed one reporter. "He lit a fire here in Springfield" (Syracuse, New York, *Herald Journal*, February 13, 1986). "I think Cuomo is probably the most charismatic governor I have encountered," said another (Syracuse *Herald American*, February 16, 1986).

Not all responses were favorable, however. William Safire, conservative syndicated columnist and former speech writer for Richard Nixon, conceded that "Cuomo's self-written speech was reverent, respectable—at times eloquent—and studded with all the right quotations," but went on to say, "the speech also was brought forth in banality, misconceived in its central theme, and dedicated to the proposition that no historian has studied the life of Lincoln since the mything of Carl Sandburg" (Providence *Journal-Bulletin*, February 17, 1986).

Mario M. Cuomo's speech: Reverend Milkman, Justice Underwood, our distinguished awardee Justice Ward, Justice Miller, Distinguished Professor Robert Johannsen, General Herrero, Dr. Curtis.

Governor Thompson, I thank you for that generous introduction. It is a privilege for Matilda and me and Christopher to be in your great state and we appreciate your taking the time to be here to introduce me.

I would also like to thank Judge Harlington Wood for inviting me to be part of this celebration of one of the monumental figures of our history, whose words and life and legend have been for me, as they have for you I'm sure, an instruction and an inspiration for most of a lifetime.

I am also honored to be in the company of Representative Richard Durbin, who occupies the congressional seat Lincoln held, and Senator Paul Simon, himself an extraordinary success story, a man of intellect and integrity, whose distinguished works on the Lincoln theme have illuminated the man we honor tonight.

It is an intimidating thing to stand here tonight to talk about the greatest intellect, the greatest leader, perhaps the greatest soul America has ever produced. To follow such legendary orators as William Jennings Bryan and Adlai Stevenson. Only a struggling student myself, to face as imposing an audience as the Lincoln scholars—tough-minded, demanding, harsh critics, highly intelligent. And to face so many Republicans: tough-minded, demanding, harsh critics . . .

And I certainly wasn't encouraged after I learned that when another New York governor, Franklin D. Roosevelt, announced his intention to come here to speak on Lincoln, a local political stalwart threatened him with an injunction.

To be honest with you, I feel a little like the Illinois man from one Lincoln story. When he was confronted by a local citizens' committee with the prospect of being tarred and feathered and run out of town on a rail, he announced, "If it weren't for the honor of the thing, I'd just as soon it happened to someone else."

I should tell you one more thing before I go on with my remarks. It would be foolish to deny that there has been some speculation surrounding this event about ambitions for the presidency. Let me be candid. I don't know anyone who wouldn't regard it as the highest possible political privilege to be President. And governors are, perhaps, better prepared than most to be President. Governors like Teddy Roosevelt and F.D.R. and even governors from places like Georgia and California, particularly governors of great industrial states with good records. That's because governors do more than make speeches. They have to make budgets and run things, and that's what Presidents do.

So, the truth is, despite what might be said about planning to run again for governor, the speculation about the Presidency is plausible. I wouldn't be a bit surprised—if the election goes well this year for him—if early next year you heard a declaration of interest from a reelected governor of a large state—Jim Thompson. Good luck, Jim!

But seriously, this is an event beyond the scope of partisan politics. When Lincoln gave his one and only speech in my capital, Albany, New York, he told the Democratic governor, "You have invited and received me without distinction of party." Let me second that sentiment, and thank you for inviting and receiving me in the same spirit.

To be here in Springfield, instead of at the memorial in Washington, to celebrate this "high holy day" of Lincoln remembrance, gives us a special advantage. In Washington, Lincoln towers far above us, presiding magisterially, in a marble temple. His stony composure, the hugeness of him there, gives him and his whole life a grandeur that places him so far above and beyond us that it's difficult to remember the reality of him. We have lifted Lincoln to the very pinnacle of our national memory, enlarged him to gargantuan proportions in white stone re-creations. We have chiseled his face on the side of a mountain, making him appear as a voice in the heavens.

There is a danger when we enshrine our heroes, when we lift them onto pedestals and lay wreaths at their feet. We can, by the very process of elevating them, strain the sense of connection between them and the palpable, fleshy, sometimes mean concerns of our own lives. It would be a terrible shame to lose Lincoln that way, to make of him a celebration but not an instruction; a memory, but not a model; a legend but not a lesson.

Here in Springfield there is less chance of that. Although he left Springfield 125 years ago, here—where he practiced law, served as a legislator, and warned this nation of the dangers of a "house divided"—Lincoln, the man, still presides. Here we can remember that Lincoln—the miracle that we call Lincoln—worked within the hard, sometimes discouraging, sometimes terrifying, limits of time and place and chance. And by our so remembering, he can again begin to light our minds and move our hearts.

That is why I have come here, not just to light a candle to the apparition of him, but to remember his specific wisdom and goodness and to consider how it can continue to touch us, to teach us, to move us to the higher ground.

I have come to remember Lincoln as he was. The flesh and blood man, haunted by mortality in his waking and his dreaming life. The boy who had been uprooted from one frontier farm to another, across Kentucky and Indiana and Illinois, by a father restless with his own dreams.

To remember some of Lincoln's own words, which, taken altogether, are the best words America has ever produced. To remember the words that he spoke ten days after his lyrical, wrenching farewell to Springfield on his way to his inauguration as our sixteenth President. "Back in my childhood," he said then, "the earliest days of my being able to read, I got hold of a small book . . . Weems' *Life of Washington*:

> I remember all the accounts there given of the battlefields and struggles for the liberties of the country and the great hardships of that time fixed themselves on . . . my memory. I recollect thinking then, boy even though I was, that there must have been something more than common that those men struggled for. I am exceedingly anxious that the thing which they struggled for; that something even more than national independence; that something that held out a promise to all the people of the world for all time to come; . . . shall be perpetuated in accordance with the original idea for which the struggle was made.

Here was Lincoln, just before his inauguration, reminding us of the source of his strength and eventual greatness, his compelling need to understand the meaning of things and to commit to a course that was directed by reason, supported by principle, designed to achieve the greatest good. He was a man of ideas, grand and soaring ones, and he was cursed by the realization that they were achievable ideas as well, so that he could not escape the obligation of pursuing them, despite the peril and the pain that pursuit would inevitably bring.

Even as a boy he grasped the great idea that would sustain him—and provoke him—for the rest of his days, the idea that took hold of his heart and his mind, the idea that he tells us about again and again throughout his life. It became the thread of purpose that tied the boy to the man to the legend—the great idea—the dream, the achievable dream, of equality, of opportunity . . . for all: "The original idea for which the struggle was made . . . " The proposition that all men are created equal, that they are endowed by their creator with certain unalienable rights, that among these are life, liberty and the pursuit of happiness.

Even by Lincoln's time, for many, the words had been heard often enough so that they became commonplace, part of the intellectual and historical landscape, losing their dimension, their significance, their profoundness.

But not for Lincoln. He pondered them, troubled over their significance, wrestled with their possibilities. "We did not learn quickly or easily that all men are created equal," one Lincoln scholar has observed. No. We did not learn those words quickly or easily. We are still struggling with them in fact, as Lincoln did for a whole lifetime. From the time he read Weems' little book until the day he was martyred, he thought, and planned, and prayed to make the words of the declaration, a way of life. Equality and opportunity, for all. But truly, for *all*.

Lincoln came to believe that the great promise of the founding fathers was one that had only begun to be realized with the founding fathers themselves. He understood that from the beginning it was a promise that would have to be fulfilled in degrees. Its embrace would have to be widened over the years, step by step, sometimes painfully, until finally it included everyone.

That was his dream. That was his vision. That was his mission. With it, he defined for himself and for us the soul of our unique experiment in government: the belief that the promise of the Declaration of Independence—the promise of equality and opportunity—cannot be considered kept, until it includes everyone.

For him, that was the unifying principle of our democracy. Without it, we had no nation worth fighting for. With it, we had no limit to the good we might achieve. He spent the rest of his life trying to give the principle meaning. He consumed himself doing it. He reaffirmed Jefferson's preference for the human interest and the human right. "The principles of Jefferson," he said, "are the definitions and axioms of free society."

But Lincoln extended those instincts to new expressions of equality. Always, he searched for ways to bring within the embrace of the new freedom, the new opportunity, all who had become Americans. Deeply—reverently—grateful for the opportunity afforded him, he was pained by the idea that it should be denied others, or limited.

He believed that the human right was more than the right to exist, to live free from oppression. He believed it included the right to achieve, to thrive, so he reached out for the "penniless beginner." He thought it the American promise that every "poor man" should be given his chance. He saw what others would or could not see: the immensity of the fundamental ideas of freedom and self-determination that made his young nation such a radically new adventure in government.

But he was not intimidated by that immensity. He was willing to use the ideas as well as to admire them, to mold them so as to apply them to new circumstances, to wield them as instruments of justice and not just echoes of it.

Some said government should do no more than protect its people from insurrection and foreign invasion and spend the rest of its time dispassionately observing the way its people played out the cards that fate had dealt them. He scorned that view. He called it a "do nothing" abdication of responsibility. "The legitimate object of government," he said, "is to do for the people what needs to be done, but which they cannot, by individual effort, do at all, or do so well, for themselves. There are many such things . . . ," he said.

So he offered the "poor" more than freedom and the encouragement of his own good example: He offered them government, government that would work aggressively to help them find the chance they might not have found alone. He did it by fighting for bridges, railroad construction, and other such projects that others decried as excessive government. He gave help for education, help for agriculture, land for the rural family struggling for a start.

And always, at the heart of this struggle and his yearning was the passion to make room for the outsider, the insistence upon a commitment to respect the idea of equality by fighting for inclusion. Early in his career, he spoke out for women's suffrage. His contempt for the "Do-Nothings" was equalled by his disdain for the "Know-Nothings."

America beckoned foreigners, but many Americans—organized around the crude selfishness of the Nativist Movement—rejected them. The Nativists sought to create two classes of people, the old stock Americans and the intruders from other places, keeping the intruders forever strangers in a strange land.

Lincoln shamed them with his understanding and his strength. "I am not a Know-Nothing," he said. "How could I be? How can anyone who abhors the oppression of Negroes be in favor of degrading classes of white people? . . . As a nation we began by declaring 'all men are created equal.'

"We now practically read it, 'All men are created equal except Negroes.' When the Know-Nothings get control, it will read 'All men are created equal except Negroes, and Catholics, and foreigners.'" Then he added: "When it comes to this I shall prefer emigrating to some country where they make no pretense of loving liberty—to Russia for instance, where despotism can be taken pure, and without the base alloy of hypocrisy."

Had Lincoln not existed, or had he been less than he was and the battle to keep the nation together had been lost, it would have meant the end of the American experiment. Secession would have bred secession, reducing us into smaller and smaller fragments until finally we were just the broken pieces of the dream.

Lincoln saved us from that. But winning the great war for unity did not preserve us from the need to fight further battles in the struggle to balance our diversity with our harmony, to keep the pieces of the mosaic intact, even while making room for new pieces. That work is today, as it was in 1863, still an unfinished work . . . still a cause that requires "a full measure of devotion."

For more than 100 years, the fight to include has continued:

—in the struggle to free working people from the oppression of a ruthless economic system that saw women and children worked to death and men born to poverty, live in poverty, and die in poverty—in spite of working all the time.

—in the continuing fight for civil rights, making Lincoln's promise real.

—in the effort to keep the farmer alive.

—in the ongoing resistance to preserve religious freedom from the arrogance of the Know-Nothing and the zealotry of those who would make their religion the state's religion.

—in the crusade to make women equal, legally and practically.

Many battles have been won. The embrace of our unity has been gradually but inexorably expanded. But Lincoln's work is not yet done.

A century after Lincoln preached his answer of equality and mutual respect, some discrimination—of class or race or sex or ethnicity—as a bar to full participation in America still remains. Unpleasant reminders of less enlightened times linger. Sometimes they are heard in whispers. At other times they are loud enough to capture the attention of the American people.

I have had my own encounter with this question and I have spoken of it. Like millions of others, I am privileged to be a first generation American. My mother and father came to this country more than sixty years ago with nothing but their hopes, without education, skills, or wealth. Through the opportunity given them here to lift themselves through hard work, they were able to raise a family. My mother has lived to see her youngest child become chief executive of one of the greatest states in the greatest nation in the only world we know.

Like millions of other children of immigrants, I know the strength that immigrants can bring. I know the richness of a society that allows us a whole new culture without requiring us to surrender the one our parents were born to. I know the miraculous power of this place that helps people rise up from poverty to security, and even affluence, in the course of a single lifetime. With generations of other children of the immigrants, I know about equality and opportunity and unity, in a special way.

And I know how, from time to time, all this beauty can be challenged by the misguided children of the Know-Nothings, by the short-sighted and the unkind, by contempt that masks itself as humor, by all the casual or conscious bigotry that must keep the American people vigilant.

We heard such voices again recently saying things like, Italians are not politically popular. Catholics will have a problem. He has an ethnic problem. An ethnic problem. We hear the word again, "Wop."

"We oftentimes refer to people of Italian descent as 'Wops'," said one public figure, unabashedly.

Now, given the unbroken string of opportunity and good fortune provided me by this great country, I might simply have ignored these references. I could easily have let the words pass as inconsequential, especially remembering Lincoln, himself the object of scorn and ridicule.

But the words, they took on significance because they were heard far beyond my home or my block or even my state, because they were heard by others who remembered times of their own when words stung and menaced them and their people. And because they raised a question about our system of fundamental American values that Lincoln helped construct and died for. Is it true? Are there really so many who have never heard Lincoln's voice, or the sweet sound of reason and fairness? So many who do not understand the beauty and power of this place, that they could make of the tint of your skin, or the sex you were born to, or the vowels of your name, an impediment to progress in this, the land of opportunity?

I believed the answer would be clear, so I asked for it by disputing the voices of division, by saying, "It is not so. It is the voice of ignorance and I challenge you to show me otherwise."

In no time at all the answer has come back from the American people, everyone saying the same things: "Of course it's wrong to judge a person by the place where his forebears came from, of course that would violate all that we stand for, fairness and common sense. It shouldn't even have been brought up. It shouldn't even have been a cause for discussion."

I agree. It should not have been. But it was. And the discussion is now concluded, with the answer I was sure of and the answer I am proud of as an American, the answer Lincoln would have given: "You will rise or fall on your merits as a person and the quality of your work. All else is distraction."

Lincoln believed, with every fibre of his being, that this place, America, could offer a dream to all mankind, different than any other in the annals of history: more generous, more compassionate, more inclusive.

No one knew better than Lincoln our sturdiness, the ability of most of us to make it on our own given the chance. But at the same time, no one knew better the idea of family, the idea that unless we helped one another, there were some who would never make it.

One person climbs the ladder of personal ambition, reaches his dream, and then turns and pulls the ladder up. Another reaches the place he has sought, turns, and reaches down for the person behind him. With Lincoln, it was that process of turning and reaching down, that commitment to keep lifting people up the ladder, which defined the American character, stamping us forever with a mission that reached even beyond our borders to embrace the world.

Lincoln's belief in America, in the American people, was broader, deeper, more daring than any other person's of his age—and, perhaps, ours, too. And this is the near-unbelievable greatness of the man, that with that belief, he not only led us, he created us.

His personal mythology became our national mythology. It is as if Homer not only chronicled the siege of Troy, but conducted the siege as well. As if Shakespeare set his playwrighting aside to lead the English against the Armada. Because Lincoln embodied his age in his actions and in his words:

—words, even and measured, hurrying across three decades, calling us to our destiny;

—words he prayed, and troubled over, more than a million words in his speeches and writings;

—words that chronicled the search for his own identity as he searched for a nation's identity;

—words that were, by turns, as chilling as the night sky and as assuring as home;

—words his reason sharpened into steel, and his heart softened into an embrace;

—words filled with all the longings of his soul and of his century;

—words wrung from his private struggle, spun to capture the struggle of a nation;

—words out of his own pain to heal that struggle;

—words of retribution, but never of revenge;

—words that judged, but never condemned;

—words that pleaded, cajoled for the one belief—that the promise must be kept—that the dream must endure and grow, until it embraces everyone;

—words ringing down into the present;

—all the hope and the pain of that epic caught, somehow, by his cadences: the tearing away, the binding together, the leaving behind, the reaching beyond.

As individuals, as a people, we are still reaching up, for a better job, a better education, a better society, even for the stars, just as Lincoln did. But because of Lincoln, we do it in a way that is unique to this world.

What other people on earth have ever claimed a quality of character that resided not in a way of speaking, dressing, dancing, praying, but in an idea? What other people on earth have ever refused to set the definitions of their identity by anything other than that idea?

No, we have not learned quickly or easily that the dream of America endures only so long as we keep faith with the struggle to include, but Lincoln—through his words and his works—has etched that message forever into our consciousness.

Lincoln showed us, for all time, what unites us. He taught us that we cannot rest until the promise of equality and opportunity embraces every region, every race, every religion, every nationality, and every class, until it includes, "the penniless beginner" and the "poor man seeking his chance."

In his time, Lincoln saw that as long as one in every seven Americans was enslaved, our identity as a people was hostage to that enslavement. He faced that injustice. He fought it. He gave his life to see it righted.

Time and again, since then, we have had to face challenges that threatened to divide us, and, time and again, we have conquered them. We reached out—hesitantly at times, sometimes only after great struggle, but always we reached out—to include impoverished immigrants, the farmer and the factory worker, women, the disabled.

To all those whose only assets were their great expectations, America found ways to meet those expectations and to create new ones. Generations of hard-working people moved into the middle class and beyond. We created a society as open and free as any on earth, and we did it Lincoln's way: by founding that society on a belief in the boundless enterprise of the American people.

Always, we have extended the promise, moving toward the light, toward our declared purpose as a people: "To form a more perfect union," to overcome all that divides us because we believe the ancient wisdom that Lincoln believed, "A house divided against itself cannot stand."

Step by step, our embrace grows wider. The old bigotries seem to be dying. The old stereotypes and hatreds, that denied so many their full share of an America they helped build, have gradually given way to acceptance, fairness, and civility.

But still, great challenges remain. Suddenly, ominously, a new one has emerged.

In Lincoln's time, one of every seven Americans was a slave. Today, for all our affluence and might, despite what every day is described as our continuing economic recovery, nearly one in every seven Americans lives in poverty, not in chains—because Lincoln saved us from that—but trapped in a cycle of despair that is its own enslavement.

Today, while so many of us do so well, one of every two minority children is born poor, many of them to be oppressed for a lifetime by inadequate education and the suffocating influence of broken families and social disorientation. Our identity as a people is hostage to the grim facts of more than 33 million Americans for whom equality and opportunity is not yet an attainable reality, but only an illusion.

Some people look at these statistics and the suffering people behind them, and deny them, pretending instead we are all one great "shining city on a hill." Lincoln told us for a lifetime—and for all time to come—that there can be no shining city when one in seven of us is denied the promise of the declaration. He tells us today that we are justly proud of all that we have accomplished, but that for all our progress, for all our achievement, for all that so properly makes us proud, we have no right to rest, content; nor justification for turning from the effort, out of fear or lack of confidence.

We have met greater challenges with fewer resources. We have faced greater perils with fewer friends. It would be a desecration of our belief and an act of ingratitude for the good fortune we have had to end the struggle for inclusion because it is over for some of us.

So, this evening, we come to pay you our respects, Mr. Lincoln, not just by recalling your words and revering your memory, which we do humbly and with great pleasure.

This evening, we offer you more, Mr. President—we offer you what you have asked us for, a continuing commitment to live your truth, to go forward painful step by painful step, enlarging the greatness of this nation with patient confidence in the ultimate justice of the people.

Because, as you have told us, Mr. President, there is no better or equal hope in the world.

THE MOST UNBELIEVABLE THING[1]

ROBERT A. NISBET[2]

The wish to reward persons who have made a significant contribution—whether it is to one's country, group, or cause—is almost universal. We honor scholars, writers, scientists, musicians, and others whose performance is deemed deserving, with prizes, awards, and citations. Such recognition commonly occurs at ceremonies designed specially to highlight the contributions of the honoree. These occasions call for a special type of speech by both the presenter of the award or prize and the recipient.

On November 22, 1985, the Ingersoll Foundation presented its third annual awards: the T. S. Eliot award for fiction, drama, poetry, essays, and literary criticism and the Richard M. Weaver award for outstanding scholarly contributions in philosophy, history, ethics, and the social and political sciences. Each award recipient received $15,000. The founda-

[1]Delivered to the Ingersoll Prizes awards banquet in the Ritz-Carlton Hotel, Chicago, Illinois, at 7 P.M. on November 22, 1985.

[2]For biographical note, see Appendix.

tion is an organization through which the Ingersoll Milling Machine Company of Rockford, Illinois, conducts its philanthropic activities in conjunction with the Rockford Institute, a conservative academic think tank which concentrates on social and cultural issues. The foundation chose Robert Nisbet, professor and author, as the recipient of the 1985 Richard M. Weaver award.

Addressing the approximately one hundred scholars, writers, and community leaders in attendance at the 1985 awards were John Agresto, acting director of the National Endowment for the Humanities; John Howard, president of both the Ingersoll Foundation and The Rockford Institute; and Thomas Fleming, editor of *Chronicles of Culture* and executive secretary of the Ingersoll Prizes.

The awards banquet began with welcoming remarks from Howard, who spoke of the vision and character of the late founding editor of *Chronicles of Culture* and the first executive secretary of the Ingersoll Prizes. Later in the awards program, the historical and cultural significance of the work of Robert Nisbet and playwright Eugene Ionesco, recipient of the T. S. Eliot award, was assessed by Dr. Fleming. He identified the work of both men as part of "the counterattack" against the materialist and dehumanizing tendencies of the modern world.

The official citation honoring Nisbet was:

> When philosophers ponder the nature of community, they will inevitably turn to the writings of Robert Nisbet. With pioneering scholarship and penetrating analysis, Professor Nisbet has explored the significance of family, neighborhood, and community—the institutions that are essential to our common life. His assessment of the challenges of modernity to these enduring patterns has defined many of the leading questions for serious students of contemporary society. Never afraid to defend an unpopular position, he has helped many to regain an appreciation for those models of social thought which transcend the statistical, the political, and the ideological. His accomplishment helps to sustain our hope for a humane social order in the coming century. (*Chronicles of Culture*, January 1986, p. 26)

In a sketch published three years earlier, *Newsweek* described Nisbet in the following terms:

> Robert Nisbet is by all odds the jolliest Jeremiah now practicing. In person, as in his books, he dwells on the dire condition of our society with unfailing zest, brightening with his style the gloomy landscape he portrays. One is apt to leave the company of this tall, ruddy, 69-year-old . . . feeling that things just cannot be as bad as he says. . . . You don't have to be a conservative to cheer as he knocks about fads like sociobiology, psychohistory, and futurology. . . . Nisbet is very much a part of today's conservative intellectual establishment. (*Newsweek*, September 27, 1982, p. 78)

Robert A. Nisbet's speech: One of Hans Christian Andersen's lesser-known stories bears the title "The Most Unbelievable Thing." A king offered a fortune to the subject who created the most unbelievable thing in the arts. Competition was intense and prolonged. When at last the day of judgment came, the jury, after inspecting all the entries, settled on a marvelous fusion of a clock and calendar, one with hundreds of moving parts, set in rare metals and crowned by precious stones. This, said the jury, is surely the most unbelievable thing. But as the king was about to ratify judgment and make the award, a competitor, insane with jealousy, came up with sledgehammer in hand and smashed the beautiful creation into a thousand pieces. The crowd was horrified. But the jury said: "Why, surely, *this* is the most unbelievable thing, to smash so perfect a work of art."

Western culture may be neither unbelievable nor perfect as a work of history. But for 2,500 years it has commanded the admiration and awe, and not seldom the covetousness, of countless peoples. Set as it is upon a small promontory of the vast Eurasian continent, Western civilization has been, from at least the fifth century B.C., the unique object of wonder for peoples from almost all parts of the world. We take nothing away from the civilizations of ancient Egypt, Persia, and China when we declare the West without serious rival as the collective culture hero in world history. For this the West has, however, paid a price: the price that is always exacted of the great and noble by the envious and covetous. From the Persians turned back at Thermopylae and then the Germanic-barbarian invaders of Rome, down to their successors, the Mongols, Muslims, and Slavs, the West has been a uniquely desirable civilization in the world: The barbarians have sought to invade it from the outside, as they still do in our day. Worse, Western civilization has had, especially in modern times, those from within whose impact upon their own civilization is hardly less than that of the barbarians beyond the walls.

There are various reasons for the West's remarkable fertility of culture, and there is no time for exploring any of them in proper measure. There is one reason, though, that I want to stress here: the West's unequaled profusion of inventions during its two and a half millennia of existence. I am referring to more than the mechanical inventions which immediately come to mind, though I do not deprecate these. Almost all cultural change has in it invention of one kind or other. This is as true of systems of morality, musical composition, statecraft, literature and its forms, and painting and sculpture as it is of technology and science. So much that we lazily ascribe to "growth" and "development" is in fact the child of Western man's inventive genius.

There is no other civilization known that can match the prodigality of inventions in the West. The reasons are several and begin with the generally freer air that has existed from the beginning. But there is one that I want particularly to note here: the conception of time in Western thought. Man is a time-binding creature, a faculty that along with language gives him uniqueness among the species. Tomorrow and tomorrow may creep into the present, but so do all our yesterdays. Nothing is more important to the creative process than the conception of the past. Cultures have become ossified from too strict a veneration for the past; but they have been turned to cultural froth by ignorance or neglect of the past. If a culture is absolutely obliged to choose, it is better to mummify the past than to be in ignorance of it. But far better, as the West's course illustrates, is the steering carefully between the Scylla of rapt immobility and the Charybdis of idle neglect. What is important is use of the past to serve the present.

The great ages of Western history, beginning with Pericles' Athens and including the High Middle Ages, and not forgetting America's 18th century, have been built around a singularly delicate but potent balancing of past and present, a balancing in which the imperatives of the present make all the brighter the rich and diverse resources of the past. There is a telescoping of the generations in such ages. St. Augustine likened the development of humanity to the education of a single individual through all time. In the 13th century an allegorical figure became common in writing: that of a dwarf standing on the shoulders of a giant. The dwarf represented the present, the giant the past. Only by availing himself of the giant could the dwarf see farther into the future than could the giant.

My own sense of individual biography suggests that the past has similar importance in the works of highly creative individuals. There is an acute feeling for what Eliot called the "usable past." Eliot's reverence for the past is best shown by his mining of it for often radical poetic purposes. From Plato to Einstein there is a continuing respect for the past, a respect that is based upon the sense of the past's richness as a mine of resources in all areas of the human mind. Max Planck, whose quantum theory is often held to be the single most revolutionary idea in 20th-century physical science, was notorious for his traditionalism; he himself said that he found the theory in materials available to everyone; and he said also that he had not turned to this new theory until every possible explanation from the past had been examined first. Churchill said that he loved the past, distrusted the present, and feared the future. A friend likened his mind to a layer-cake, each layer an epoch of the past. For all that, Churchill's grasp of the present was, as we know gratefully, superior. The greater of the Impressionists knew and respected the past; they sought only to build on it by use of inventions in color. Had it not been for a blockheaded establishment in Paris, fearful of all innovation in art, the Impressionists would have shown their canvases in conventional galleries; and their true relation to the past would have been instantly evident.

The most unbelievable thing about the 20th century is the near-loss of the past: loss through crippling and distortion, often through its murder. Quite rightly does the historian J. H. Plumb refer to "the death of the past." Eliot speaks of "disowning the past." Our conception of present and past is no longer the dwarf standing on a giant's shoulders. In our art and literature and philosophy, the dwarf has gotten down from the giant, to stand on the ground and kick the giant's ankles. Our flouting of the past is exactly commensurate with our narcissism of the present and our worship of the future. The greatest crime the intellectual can be thought guilty of is that of treating the past with respect, of "romanticizing the past" as convention and cant usually have it. Nostalgia, which is the rust of memory, is permitted because it sells well; but not history. Hence, as everyone knows, the scuttling of curriculum in the schools by undermining the study of history. Never would the NEA [National Education Association] "turn the clock back," as they love to say.

Such undermining is far from being merely a conceit of schools of education. It stems from our transformed popular regard for the past. For at least three centuries in the West there has been a relentless growth of systems of thought based upon a proposed extermination of the past from human thought. Descartes' rationalism, which has been well called "intellectual terrorism," urged the burning of all libraries and museums; Rousseau drew from this Cartesian philosophical nihilism a program of all-out political nihilism; Marx, child of both Descartes and Rousseau, saw all history as the necessary destruction of the past, in the interest of an ever-evolving present. And Freud populated the racial past with mythologically derived demons which relegate memory and tradition to the bins of the unconscious.

But for all the assaults of modern Western history, the past is fundamentally indestructible. As I said, man is a time-binding creature; he can no more live without the past in his contemplation of the present than he can live without oxygen. The past is inseparable from the creative process and also from simple adaptation to crisis. The single greatest message of Orwell's *1984* is the tribute paid to the past by its incessant distortion by the totalitarian masters. The Bolsheviks, determined at first to create the new Soviet man overnight and to wipe out the Russian past, were not long in discovering the value of linking the Communist present to the pasts of Novgorod, Kiev, and the courts of Ivan and Peter. Over and over the lesson is the same: Cast the past out the front door, as did Descartes, Rousseau, and Marx, and it will enter the side door. Inasmuch as the future is absolutely dark to our eyes and is the abode of charlatans, we have only the past to go to when we seek relief from the frustrations of the present. Not to the past of nostalgics, romantics, and antiquarians, but the past that is a vast theater in time with innumerable human dramas from which to draw inspiration and even role-models.

Someone, I think it was Camus, conceived the parable of the bee. It is in man's power, the parable says, to destroy the bee with a single clench of his hand. But the bee's sting has kept it alive as a species for 50 million years. It is the sting of the neglected past that will surely force us to restore it to the high place our forefathers gave it. And this will not be long in coming, I firmly believe.

SHAPING THE FUTURE

VICTIMS OF MISPLACED CONFIDENCE: TECHNOLOGY AND VALUES[1]

ALLAN H. CLARK[2]

The remarkable breakthroughs and advances in science and technology in our time have led many people to believe that any problem can be solved if only the experts put their minds to it. Dr. Allan H. Clark, who was dean of the School of Science at Purdue University, explored these high expectations in a speech he delivered to the sixth annual conference for businessmen sponsored by the Indiana Committee for the Humanities on April 22, 1985. Clark observed that

> We expect continued progress in medicine with eventual cures for all diseases as well as bionic replacements for worn-out parts. . . . We expect the ingenuity of American free enterprise to devise a never-ending parade of new products and techniques to maintain our status as the world's richest nation. . . .
> Most important of all, we expect an arsenal of weapons to make us secure and a defensive shield against ICBM's that will render nuclear weapons obsolete.

"That is a tall order," Clark concluded. He then stated the purpose of his address: "I want to persuade you that if we place all our trust in technology to solve the world's problems, we will make ourselves the victims of misplaced confidence."

Clark proceeded to examine the contributions and limitations of scientific research in medicine, food production, population control, economic growth, and defense. "We have come a long way with technological progress," he acknowledged, noting that "what security and well-being we have we owe to its products." He warned, however, that "if we are to continue that progress and achieve the full promise of technology, we need to keep a realistic view of what technology can do." A realistic view, he told his listeners, included the recognition that:

> To do the job right requires more than just technical expertise. We need common sense, and what is more, we need faith, hope, and charity—the gifts of the spirit. We must place our confidence in men as well as machines, in human character as well as human intelligence. Then should we be the victims of misplaced confidence, there is not any hope for us. And never was.

[1]Delivered before the Indiana Committee for the Humanities, Seasons Lodge and Conference Center, Nashville, Indiana, at a breakfast meeting at 8:30 A.M. on April 22, 1985.

[2]For biographical note, see Appendix.

The fact that Clark was a professor and dean of the School of Science at a large and prestigious Indiana university (he has since become president of Clarkson University in Potsdam, New York) undoubtedly contributed to his credibility with his audience, which consisted of approximately 150 small-business people from around the state of Indiana. The group also included academics from the humanities, who participated in a question and answer period after the speech.

Allan H. Clark's speech: Some time ago the following classified advertisement appeared in the *New York Times*: "Dr. Cooper, 14 Duane St., may be consulted on all diseases of a private nature. A practice of 32 years devoted to the treatment of diseases of a delicate nature enables Dr. Cooper to make speedy cures. The victims of misplaced confidence can call with the certainty of being cured." On the 3rd of July 1868, when this ad appeared, no one regarded medical advertising as unethical. Even so, Dr. Cooper was guilty of fraud. The syphilitic patient who consulted Dr. Cooper could look forward to a painful and sometimes fatal treatment with compounds of mercury. The motto of the day was "One night with Venus, a lifetime with Mercury."

The patient who consulted Dr. Cooper had little knowledge of venereal disease and less idea of how to avoid it. Sage advice of the day stressed the evil of "solitary vice" as it was called, insisting that it caused everything from bashfulness to insanity.

Dr. Cooper would have administered mercuric or mercurous chloride orally, topically, or by intramuscular injection. When the symptoms subsided, he claimed credit. Neither he nor any other physician knew about the long latency period in syphilis or the tertiary stage which follows, bringing insanity, heart disease, and death. Everyone who consulted Dr. Cooper was a victim of misplaced confidence.

No effective treatment of syphilis existed until 1908 when Paul Ehrlich discovered his famous "magic bullet," arsphenamine, the first effective agent against a microbial disease. However, treatment was arduous, requiring a long series of painful injections with devastating side effects. Most patients did not last the course.

"What do you give the man who has everyone?" Penicillin. As most of you know, syphilis responds well to low doses of penicillin, the first antibiotic. Discovered in 1929 by Sir Arthur Fleming, penicillin was developed into a safe and effective treatment for bacterial diseases in World War II. When it was introduced against syphilis in 1944, the incidence was 447 cases per 100,000 population in the United States. By 1960 the incidence was 68 cases per 100,000. It has risen slightly since that time, probably due to freer sexual behavior.

The success of penicillin led to the development of other antibiotics effective against a variety of diseases. Medicine was able to cure diseases rather than just ameliorate symptoms until the disease or the patient succumbed. A huge pharmaceutical business developed in the succeeding decades.

I have four reasons for citing this story as an example of technological progress. First, it has all the important elements: a problem of social significance, dramatically and decisively resolved by basic scientific discoveries, pushed to practical effect by military needs, finally resulting in large commercial enterprise. Second, it reminds us that technological progress is not confined to mechanical and electrical science. Third, it offers an example where economics was neither the driving force nor the principal benefit. Finally, it is a success story in an area where we pride ourselves with justification on tremendous achievement. Medicine may be the best—certainly it is the most familiar—example of applied science.

We have high expectations of technology. We do physical labor only as recreation. My children won't do even that; scratching is all they are willing to do by hand. None of us expects to grow our own food; nor do we expect food shortages or the great seasonal variations in diet that our grandparents knew. We are surprised that hunger is a problem for anyone in a country where overproduction is the chief agricultural concern.

We expect continued progress in medicine with eventual cures for all diseases as well as bionic replacements for worn-out parts. These days medicine can make you a new man or a new woman; the choice is yours. The artificial heart, the perfect metaphor for this technological age, has been this year's big news—not only the one implanted in William Schrader, but also the one David Stockman was born with. As a result of safe, effective, and inexpensive birth control, everyone can count on the desired 2.4 children.

We expect the ingenuity of American free enterprise to devise a never-ending parade of new products and techniques to maintain our status as the world's richest nation. We expect to export these products and the technology for profit and for the well-being of our fellow humans. Most important of all, we expect an arsenal of weapons to make us secure and a defensive shield against ICBM's that will render nuclear weapons obsolete.

This is a tall order. I want to persuade you that if we place all our trust in technology to solve the world's problems, we will make ourselves the victims of misplaced confidence.

Since I began with a medical example, let's first consider the problem of disease worldwide. A case can be made that medicine became a science only in this century. The development of antibiotics which began with penicillin is the great medical triumph of our time, and the first true cure of disease. We have eliminated smallpox worldwide through a quarter century campaign that began in 1958. (However the victory is still too recent to be fully certified.)

Even the successes against bacterial diseases remain partial. In recent years the leprosy bacterium has grown resistant to antibiotics. Tuberculosis, syphilis, diphtheria, tetanus, and dysentery remain horrendous problems throughout much of the world. The recent epidemic of salmonellosis shows that even in highly developed countries constant vigilance is required.

The common cold is not the only thing medicine can't cure. No virus disease is curable. Some, like polio, are preventable; some, like colds, run their course doing little harm; some, like influenza, can be treated symptomatically. But cure we cannot.

Viruses, the smallest microorganisms, too small to reproduce independently, must infiltrate a cell and replicate with cell division. They are hard to get at: Physically they are small, but chemically they are large. Worse than that, they are the most genetically variable of nature's creations and evolve rapidly. This accounts for the continuing menace of influenza around the world. The same virus may cause more than one disease: chickenpox in children and shingles in adults. Viruses are important causes of cancer and "slow viruses" are implicated in autoimmune diseases such as multiple sclerosis and myasthenia gravis.

Acquired Immune Deficiency Syndrome is caused by a virus, HTLV-III, and may have originated in African monkeys years ago. Although centered in the community of male homosexuals for the moment, like other fashions from the gay world, it will soon vector into the whole population. Already it has shown signs of evolving. It is a serious threat to world health, yet so far the only federal funds spent in the United States have been taken from research on Hepatitis B. It is hard to imagine a policy more dangerous or more stupid. It would be absurd if after all these years of avoiding nuclear war, the human race was destroyed by a virus.

In warmer climates cholera, leprosy, schistosomiasis, yaws, and many other diseases are rampant. It is estimated that malaria infects 100% of African children by their third year. Dysentery is common: Houseflies which take 44 days to develop from embryo to adult in temperate climates, take only 10 days in the tropics. Life expectancy at birth in the developing nations of Africa is less than 45 years.

In brief, the problem of disease alone is overwhelming in its complexity. However, for the sake of argument let us suppose that we could solve health problems around the world at least to the extent of raising standards of medical care to the level prevailing in this country. What would be the effect in addition to the increase in country clubs?

Certainly such an achievement would exacerbate a worldwide food shortage that has reached crisis. Africa's food production per capita has declined 11% since 1970 due to population increases. Worldwide grain reserves have been reduced from an 88-day supply in 1960 to a 46-day supply last year. By the end of the century, it will further diminish to 22 days. This provides little margin for variations of temperature and precipitation.

What about population control? The terrifying fact is that 60% of the world's population live in countries with high population growth and less than 6% in countries with zero population growth. For many years the U.S. promoted birth control to developing nations who resisted it—for a variety of cultural and political reasons. Now that the developing nations have accepted birth control, we have changed our position. We now tell them that sound economic development is the key to population control. We have withdrawn all support that could conceivably be used for coercive birth control or abortion. The United States representative to the Mexico City conference last year told a gathering of 149 nations that "the relationship between population growth and economic development is not necessarily a negative one. More people do not necessarily mean less growth." In other words our policy is that more growth will mean less people. We are going to take away the pills and pass out copies of *The Search for Excellence*.

What about economic growth then as a product of technology? Is it possible that sufficient growth could be achieved to solve the health and population problems of the world? It is hard to envision conditions that would permit this. Although consumption of oil has decreased from its all-time high in 1979, we still use three times as much oil per capita today as we did in 1950. To supply enough energy to transport raw materials and finished products in developing nations is only a dream at present. Nuclear power is a fading dream, a technology we have all but thrown away through graft and greed. By the end of this century nuclear power will be the most expensive source of energy.

If we solved the health problems, we would be left with gigantic problems in population control and economic development, problems requiring enormous resources. Unfortunately those resources are used for military expenditures.

World military expenditures increased 40 percent in constant dollars from 1973 to 1983, taking up 6 percent of the world's gross product and more than one fifth of its science and technology effort. Two of every nine research workers around the world are engaged in military projects. The United States spends 6 percent of its gross product on defense and the Soviet Union 9 percent. This diversion of capital into military expenditures has helped to make the Soviet Union the world's largest importer of food. It is reassuring to know that if the Russians attack us, they will suffer a terrible grain shortage.

All right, we can't rely on technology to solve the world's medical, population, or economic problems. Surely we can count on technology to defend us. This must be the one area where technology reigns supreme. In *Man and Superman* George Bernard Shaw wrote:

> I tell you that in the arts of life man invents nothing; but in the arts of death he outdoes Nature herself, and produces by chemistry and machinery all the slaughter of plague, pestilence, and famine. . . . There is nothing in man's industrial machinery but his greed and sloth: His heart is in his weapons. . . . Man measures his strength by his destructiveness.

The modern military man has an impressive array of armaments at his disposal; for example the Division Air Defense gun, known as DIVAD. This weapon uses the doppler effect to identify objects and aim its twin barrels automatically. In a test DIVAD ignored the drone helicopter presented to it and instead locked in on a portable latrine, whose exhaust fan provided a more attractive signal.

The computerization and electronic gadgeteering of traditional weapons has progressed so far that not only is field repair out of the question, but even field operation by the ordinary serviceman is questionable. The AR-15 was a perfectly good civilian automatic rifle. The Army set out to improve its fire power and produced the renowned M-16 which jammed excessively. The Air Force plans construction of an Advanced Tactical Fighter with flight characteristics that verge so close to instability that a computer is required to fly it—manual flight will be impossible. Now I ask you, what could possibly go wrong?

Well, does it matter? Nuclear weapons are our principal defense. The centerpiece of our preparedness is the ICBM. In one film after another we see mock-ups of the missile control center, huge screens showing the exact position of incoming missiles, grimly competent generals on the red phone to the White House. Such a control center exists at Cheyenne Mountain in Colorado. Daniel Ford, who wrote the recent two-part article in the *New Yorker* entitled "The Button," asked Brigadier General Paul Wagoner to demonstrate this hot line to the White House. Wagoner picked up the phone and waited. And waited. And waited. Nothing happened. Pressed for an explanation, Wagoner later confessed, "I didn't know I had to dial 0 for the operator."

Our current deficit of $200 billion can be read as the sum of two numbers: the increase in the defense budget and the increase in debt service from deficits added in the last four years. (This is probably not the Republican party line.) The proposed budget this year has a total of $60 billion for research and development, of which $40 billion will go for military R&D.

Soon, if not already, Soviet and American missiles will have sufficient accuracy to eliminate an ICBM response from the other side. This is why the Soviets have declared the MX a first strike weapon. It is, but then so are the Soviet missiles. Our proposed counter is Star Wars, the Strategic Defense Initiative. In short, with enormous expenditure, perhaps as much as $300 billion, we hope to have, in a few decades, a defensive shield which is partially effective against Soviet ICBM's. Missiles launched from submarines or airplanes would remain a threat.

Our current nuclear arms policies are clearly insane, but we pretend not to know this. War is the worst social disease. We will all be victims of misplaced confidence if we assume technology is the cure for war.

We have come a long way with technological progress. What security and well-being we have we owe to its products. If we are to continue that progress and achieve the full promise of technology, we need to keep a realistic view of what technology can do. In summary, we need to recognize that:

1. The problems facing the world are immense and more technically difficult than we have supposed. Their solution will be slow and incomplete.

2. Even where the technological prerequisites are now available, human error as well as cultural, political, and social factors inhibit their use. Patience and perseverance will be required.

3. In any case, the developed nations devote far too large a fraction of their resources to military expenditures to have much left for their own social programs, let alone those of the underdeveloped world. Real progress depends on ending the arms race.

We need technological expertise, but we need common sense as well. Karl Taylor Compton, the famous physicist, told of his sister, who lived in India, hiring an electrician to make improvements in her home. Unable to explain herself, she said, "Oh, you know what's needed here, just use common sense and do it." To which he replied, "Alas, madam, common sense is a great gift of God. I am a humble soul with only a technical education."

To do the job right always requires more than just technical expertise. We need common sense, and what is more, we need faith, hope, and charity—the gifts of the spirit. We must place our confidence in men as well as machines, in human character as well as human intelligence. Then should we be the victims of misplaced confidence, there is not any hope for us. And never was.

AMERICA'S LIABILITY EXPLOSION: CAN WE AFFORD THE COST?[1]

ROBERT H. MALOTT[2]

On October 10, 1985, Robert H. Malott, chairman and chief executive officer of the FMC Corporation, addressed the 24th annual Corporate Council Institute, a continuing legal education program sponsored by the Northwestern University School of Law, on what he and others regard as an increasingly serious problem: "the destructive and rapidly escalating trend toward liability litigation in this country and the implications that this trend portends not only for industry but for society as a whole." To emphasize his concern, Malott stressed that liability litigation "mania"

> is costing the American public billions of dollars each year; it is undermining the competitiveness of U.S. industry; and it is threatening the very existence of some businesses in this country. Yet it is a trend that the vast majority of the American people has either failed to understand or has persistently chosen to ignore.

Malott followed a problem-solution method in organizing his speech. He began by emphasizing the problem, saying,

> The disturbing truth is that America has become the most litigious society in the world. Last year, one out of fifteen Americans filed a private civil lawsuit of some kind. In all, over 13 million private civil law suits were filed in state and federal courts.

"In some instances, the grounds for resorting to litigation strain credulity," he stated, citing "Believe It or Not"-like examples to support his contention. Malott then moved on to an examination of the causes of the problem and its effects, asking, "Who ends up paying for our current mania for litigation?" and answering, "It's obvious that we all do."

Having developed the scope of the problem and its causes and effects, the executive then proposed his solution. Following the traditional John Dewey pattern for problem-solving, Malott concluded with a strong appeal for implementing his proposals:

> I challenge all of you, as leaders in the legal profession, to join the fight for product liability law reform. . . . I urge you to stand up and be counted. . . . Above all, I urge you to make it an issue with your congressman.

Malott delivered his address to an audience of 452, most of whom were corporate or law firm attorneys.

[1]Delivered to the Corporate Counsel Institute of the Northwestern University Law School at a luncheon meeting in the ballroom of the Ritz-Carlton Hotel in Chicago on October 10, 1985.

[2]For biographical note, see Appendix.

Robert H. Malott's speech: I am delighted to have this opportunity to discuss a concern that is uppermost in my mind—namely, the destructive and rapidly escalating trend toward liability litigation in this country and the implications that this trend portends not only for industry but for society as a whole.

It is a trend that is costing the American public billions of dollars each year; it is undermining the competitiveness of U.S. industry; and it is threatening the very existence of some businesses in this country. Yet it is a trend that the vast majority of the American people has either failed to understand or has persistently chosen to ignore.

The disturbing truth is that America has become the most litigious society in the world. Last year, one out of fifteen Americans filed a private civil lawsuit of some kind. In all, over 13 million private civil law suits were filed in state and federal courts.

No less than the highest court in the land is appalled at the situation. As Chief Justice Warren Burger lamented in a recent speech, our society today "has an almost irrational focus—virtually a mania—on litigation as the way to solve all problems."

In some instances, the grounds for resorting to litigation strain credulity. Let me cite just a few examples that sound more like stories out of Ripley's "Believe It or Not" than examples of responsible American jurisprudence:

Item: Two Maryland men decided to dry their hot air balloon in a commercial laundry dryer. The dryer exploded, injuring them. They sued the manufacturer of the dryer and ended up winning nearly $900,000 in damages.

Item: An overweight man with a history of coronary disease suffered a heart attack while trying to start a Sears lawnmower. He sued Sears, charging that too much force was required to yank the mower's pull rope. A jury in Pennsylvania awarded him one million dollars, plus another $500,000 in prejudgment interest.

Item: A two-year-old child being treated in the hospital for bronchial spasms suffered brain damage from a drug overdose. Although the hospital staff had clearly exceeded the dosage level prescribed by both the attending doctor and the drug manufacturer, the child's parents successfully sued the company producing the drug. The jury award? Nine million dollars in compensation and $13 million in punitive damages.

If you think these are isolated cases of absurdly generous liability awards, you are wrong. Last year, awards of a million dollars or more were given in more than 360 personal injury suits—an incredible 13 times the number 10 years ago. The list of those afflicted by liability litigation runs the full spectrum of American business.

What is causing the problem? I attribute the current situation to the following: first, the ambiguity of current liability laws; second, an increasing acceptance of the concept of victims' *entitlement* to compensation; and third, the contingency system for compensating the legal profession.

Since the early 1960s, the concept of liability for product-related injuries has been relentlessly expanded by both state and federal courts.

First, the courts created a new legal theory, strict liability, to enable claimants to recover damages for injuries caused by defectively manufactured products. This happened because the courts believed that business, rather than the injured party, should bear the cost of manufacturing errors, regardless of fault.

Then, the concept of strict liability was extended from defects in manufacturing to defects in a particular product's design, in its operating instructions, or in its safety warnings. In essence, the focus of product liability was shifted from the conduct of manufacturers to the condition of the product itself.

However, unlike the test for manufacturing defects, there are no clear-cut standards to guide judicial decisions on the adequacy of a product's design or its safety warnings. Although some 30 states have now enacted product liability statutes, no two are alike. Consequently, cases based on similar facts, but tried in different states, can produce strikingly different and often contradictory judgments.

In an FMC case concerning a construction worker who had driven a crane into high voltage lines, an Illinois court ruled *against* FMC for not providing adequate safety warnings and for not installing automatic warning devices, even though the devices available at the time the crane was manufactured were not reliable.

Yet courts in two other states, in similar cases, ruled that the crane manufacturers were *not* liable, because the hazard of driving a steel boom into electrical lines was obvious. Any resulting injury was therefore the responsibility of the crane operator.

Such inconsistency in product liability judgments has produced enormous confusion among manufacturers and consumers alike, with neither side knowing what rights or responsibilities they have and what limits, if any, there are on liability.

Another factor contributing to the chaos in liability law is the growing "attitude of entitlement" in compensating injury victims, even in those cases where it is obvious that the manufacturer cannot be charged with responsibility or, at a minimum, responsibility is shared between the manufacturer and the injured party.

A decade ago, injured persons whose own carelessness was responsible for injury could not successfully prosecute. However, since the mid-1970s, 10 states have adopted comparative fault standards, which allow plaintiffs to recover damages even if they share responsibility for their injuries. By adopting the concept of comparative fault, these states have precipitated a whole new generation of lawsuits and are encouraging increasing numbers of people to seek compensation through suit or the threat of litigation.

Underlying this attitude toward victims' compensation is the assumption that the insurance industry, fed by corporate premiums, has a bottomless pool of funds to compensate the injured, no matter how tenuous their claims. Indeed, in some cases, courts and juries have seemed far more concerned with compensating the plaintiffs than in establishing the liability of the manufacturer.

Witness the recent litigation over Agent Orange. The judge pressured the seven corporate defendants to pay $180 million in death and disability compensation to Vietnam veterans and their families even though, as he said later, he did not believe there was any medical evidence to support their claims.

The third factor contributing to the number and cost of liability claims is the contingency system for determining legal fees.

Because plaintiffs do not incur liability by initiating action, they are encouraged to pursue injury suits even if the evidence for their claims may be relatively weak. Similarly, with liability awards now reaching a million dollars or more, lawyers have a powerful incentive to keep filing liability cases, even if the prospect of winning any one case is highly uncertain. In short, by eliminating the financial risk of bringing a case to trial, contingency fees are encouraging both plaintiffs and trial lawyers to clog the courts with suits.

In addition, contingency fees tend to increase the size of injury awards, as juries factor in the cost of legal counsel when determining the total size of damages for the plaintiff. This cost is far from insignificant.

Indeed, if one considers the legal fees for both plaintiff and defendant, it becomes clear that more money is being paid today to adjudicate a claim than the compensation being paid to victims.

According to a study by the Rand Institute for Civil Justice, only 37 percent of the amounts paid for compensation and legal fees typically goes to the claimant. The balance—or 63 percent of the assessed damages—goes to pay the legal fees of the litigants.

Because of high contingency fees and the potential for lucrative awards, liability lawyers have an enormous stake in preserving the status quo. I can assure you the plaintiffs' bar is well aware of this and is effectively organized to resist change.

Who ends up paying for our current mania for litigation? It's obvious that we all do. The growing tide of liability litigation is imposing enormous costs on consumers, on business, and on society as a whole.

As consumers, we are paying not only through higher product prices but also through the reduced availability of many products and services. Already, astronomical legal settlements and escalating insurance premiums have forced more than a few companies to drop product lines or, in some cases, to go out of business.

This trend is cutting across all segments of U.S. industry, as the following examples illustrate:

In the past decade, 10 of the 13 U.S. firms making football helmets have had to stop production, due to runaway jury awards.

In 1983, Merrell Dow was forced to discontinue production of the drug Bendectin, although the Food and Drug Administration approved the drug for treating women who suffered nausea during pregnancy. The reason? The cost of liability insurance for making Bendectin had reached 10 million dollars a year, or over 80 percent of the company's annual sales from the drug.

And today, the continued production of small aircraft in this country is being seriously threatened by burgeoning liability costs. This year, those costs to general aviation airframe manufacturers will amount to $100 million, requiring an average increase of $50,000—or 50 percent—to the cost of the average plane. Such cost increases have already led one manufacturer, Beech

Aircraft Corporation, to shut down its plant in Wichita, Kansas, and eliminate up to 12,000 jobs.

Perhaps the most pernicious example of this trend is the decline in production of the DPT vaccine, which is used to prevent diphtheria, tetanus, and pertussis—commonly known as whooping cough—among young children.

Since the introduction of the vaccine in the 1920's, the number of deaths in the United States from pertussis each year has declined dramatically from one in 10,000 to one in 10 million. Yet, nearly a dozen companies have dropped out of the DPT market in the last ten years, leaving only one U.S. producer of the vaccine and creating dangerous nationwide shortages. The reason? Excessive liability costs.

The problem is that the courts focus on compensating the pain and suffering of those injured—not on serving the needs of society as a whole. This attitude is not only adversely affecting the American public but is significantly increasing the costs of doing business for many U.S. companies and undermining their ability to compete. According to a study by the Commerce Department last year, the insurance costs that U.S. companies face for product liability coverage are many times higher than those facing manufacturers in Europe and Japan. In fact, some U.S. manufacturers of machine tools and textile machinery must support liability premiums that are 20 to 100 times greater than those paid by their foreign competitors.

FMC's own experience corroborates this. Over the last five years, our total insurance expenses in the United States, including self-insured losses, have cost five times as much as our insurance premiums in international markets. These differences in liability costs can create a major competitive disadvantage for domestic manufacturers in both local and foreign markets.

For some companies, the costs of product liability litigation are not only hurting their ability to compete, but are forcing them to seek refuge under Chapter 11 of the federal bankruptcy laws. Since the Manville Corporation made history in 1982 by declaring bankruptcy at least three other companies have followed suit.

In 1983, the James Hunter Machine Company, a small Massachusetts manufacturer of textile machinery, was forced to file for bankruptcy after being in business for 136 years because it faced liability claims totaling over $17 million.

Last year, Aquaslide 'N' Dive Corporation, the nation's largest manufacturer of diving boards and swimming pool slides, also sought protection under federal bankruptcy laws, because it did not have enough insurance or assets to cover potential liability claims.

Most recently, the A. H. Robins Company has filed for bankruptcy, due to liability suits for injuries related to the Dalkon Shield, the intrauterine birth control device the company removed from the market in 1974. By July of this year, Robins had already paid nearly $500 million in awards, settlements, and legal expenses to dispose of approximately 9,000 liability suits. Yet another 5,000 claims are still pending and more are expected.

This situation is absurd. How many more companies must be forced into Chapter 11 before we realize that it is time to revamp our liability laws? We are rapidly approaching the point where the competitive ability of U.S. manufacturers is being determined more by the vagaries of state laws and jury awards than by the price or quality of their products.

In considering potential areas for reform, it is instructive to compare our system of liability with that prevailing in Western Europe and Japan, where the incidence of product liability claims is far lower and the average size of awards is much smaller. In my view, there are three factors that account for these differences in the frequency and cost of liability litigation.

First, contingency fee arrangements are not allowed in Western Europe or Japan. Instead, plaintiffs must pay their attorneys during the course of litigation and they risk paying the legal costs for the defense if they lose.

Second, damage awards in Europe and Japan usually only cover actual expenses and loss of income. Punitive damages and awards for pain and suffering are not readily available in Europe, and they are nonexistent in Japan.

As a result, plaintiffs must bear a significant financial risk in bringing a case to trial, and generally they have lower expectations for awards. Those two factors alone act as a major disincentive to litigation.

Third, and most important, the Europeans and the Japanese have a totally different attitude toward litigation than do Americans.

Europeans generally believe that, if a product is made safely, it is up to the consumer to use it safely. The Japanese are even more conservative in their approach to litigation. They rarely use the legal system to resolve disputes and, in fact, tend to consider litigation as a form of harassment.

In contrast, Americans tend to be keenly aware of the availability of legal redress for accidental injury and appear to be willing to pursue such a course without reservation. They rely on the courts not only to settle disputes, but also to provide extensive compensation for injuries, often with little regard for who is at fault and with *no* regard for the costs they are imposing on business and society.

In my opinion, this litigation mentality cannot continue. The costs have simply become too great. Our runaway liability is contributing significantly to the competing claims of different interest groups or subordinated to other, more pressing issues on the congressional agenda.

Efforts to gain support for product liability reform in the American Bar Association have also been blocked, first at the San Francisco convention two years ago and more recently in New Orleans. This has been largely due to the enormous influence of the trial bar.

I challenge all of you, as leaders in the legal profession, to join the fight for product liability law reform. We need your help to broaden public awareness of the current crisis in product liability but, even more importantly, we need your help to counteract the political power of the trial lawyers. As vigorous supporters of the status quo, they have placed a virtual stranglehold on efforts to enact federal product liability legislation—and given the legal profession an unfortunate reputation for being more concerned with protecting its own interests than with serving the interests of society as a whole.

I urge you to stand up and be counted. Make product liability reform an issue within your company, with your trade associations, and with your outside counsel. Let them know why the issue is important to you and why it should be important to them.

Above all, I urge you to make it an issue with your congressmen. It is imperative that we maintain pressure in Washington for federal preemption. If Congress keeps brushing the issue aside, we will continue to see increasing numbers of U.S. companies succumbing to the weight of excessive litigation, exorbitant legal fees, and escalating damage awards. That is a price we can no longer afford. The time to bring our runaway liability system under control is now.

CHILDREN'S TELEVISION: A NATIONAL DISGRACE[1]

GEORGE GERBNER[2]

Dr. George Gerbner, dean of the Annenberg School of Communication at the University of Pennsylvania, delivered the keynote address at the Yale University School of Medicine symposium, "Television and Children: Facts vs. Fiction," on October 3, 1985. From the very outset, Gerbner made his position clear. He titled the speech, "Children's Television: A National Disgrace," and later described American television programming for youngsters as a "national disgrace of world-class proportions."

Gerbner began by previewing the five steps he would take to reach his conclusion. As one of the most important steps he explained what the age of television means:

> Television presents a common world to all our people, the only common denominator in an otherwise heterogeneous nation, the first true melting pot of our country. That common world is the largest single source of information.

Gerbner identified some general features of the "common world" television creates. He observed that

> For the first time in history children are born into a symbolic world that does not originate with parents, church, or school, and requires no literacy. Television has replaced most stories told by parents, and has either replaced or reorganized what we learn in school or in church. It has become the norm, the standard to which we all have to relate. We use it as a measure of our own behavior and of the behavior of people around us. We use it as a way of defining ourselves. Even if you don't watch television, you get it through other people who do.

Gerbner went on to criticize the violence of television shows, their underrepresentation of women, minorities, and senior citizens, and the general lack of quality children's programming.

The speech was delivered extemporaneously to an audience of about 225 in the School of Medicine's Mary S. Harkness auditorium. Participants in the conference, which was sponsored by the National Pediatric Association, included medical practitioners, academics, and media representatives. Other speakers included pediatrician Dr. Benjamin Spock and

[1]Keynote address delivered at 11:00 A.M., October 3, 1985, to the "Television and Children: Facts vs. Fiction" symposium, Mary S. Harkness auditorium, School of Medicine, Yale University, New Haven, Connecticut.

[2]For biographical note, see Appendix.

the president and founder of Action for Children's Television, Peggy Charren. The meeting was reported by the Associated Press and the *Washington Post* and other newspapers.

George Gerbner's speech: I'd like to reach my destination in five steps and I'll tell you what they are so you can keep me on course. First, I'd like to make some comments about what I think the age of television means. Secondly, I'd like to describe its main characteristics. Third, I will present some highlights of our research of eighteen years' standing, an ongoing project attempting to analyze the symbolic environment into which our children are born and in which they grow up. Fourth, I'd like to focus attention on so-called children's television, and I say "so-called" because only one-fifth of children's viewing goes into children's television. For the first time in human history children are plunged into an accelerated version of the adult cultural environment. I don't think we've ever fully grasped the significance of that. And fifth, I want to make some comments about the political situation that surrounds the issues we are talking about.

So now to begin. You must have heard the story about the teacher who asked, "Children, what does this century owe Thomas Edison?" One child raised his hand and spoke and said, "Teacher, without Edison we would still be watching television by candlelight!"

It is inconceivable to most of our children and grandchildren that there was an age before television. Television has become as much a fabric of our life as a pre-industrial religion and ritual must have been. Television has ushered in not just another medium but a new era. It has created a new symbolic environment into which our children are born.

The significance of that symbolic environment can be best reflected in the word that to me sums up the most distinctive element of human life, the most crucial distinction between humans and other creatures, and that word is storytelling. We experience the world through our stories about it. Whoever tells stories of a culture defines the terms and the agenda of human discourse and the issues we face in common.

There are three major ways in which human beings have told stories throughout our history. The first and certainly most lasting period, the pre-industrial, was a period of face-to-face storytelling. There was no way of saying, "Well, I don't have to tell you about this, you can look it up." Stories about the origin of life, the nature of the universe, and the modes of right and wrong conduct had to be remembered, rehearsed, and repeated in something we now call ritual mythology, even religion.

It was only relatively recently, with the coming of the industrial revolution, that the method of storytelling has changed. The first mechanical device putting out standardized commodities, the first machine, was the printing press. The first manufactured commodity was the book. Indeed, that was necessary for all the rest of the upheavals of the industrial revolution to come.

With the book you record and mass-produce the stories of the culture. You make it possible for people to get off the land, to go into other countries and continents, and to take much of their culture, much of their world, much of their mythology, much of their community with them. The book breaks up the ritual. It ushers in the Reformation. It makes it possible for people to go anywhere in the world and no longer be dependent on the local culture. The ministration of the chief or the priest is no longer necessary just to convey the word. The early Protestants could say, "Here is the Book, read it for yourself." Others could say: take it with you, develop your own interpretation, your own tastes. Different cultures, different religions could begin to live side by side.

The book made possible the plurality of storytelling, the plurality of "worlds" that storytelling builds for different people.

A modern mass public is a community that never meets face-to-face. It is created through publication. The notion of self-government itself is predicated on the ability to be reasonably free, to cultivate competing and conflicting conceptions of life of society side by side, competing for attention, competing for support, competing for votes.

In the last forty years or so, the situation has fundamentally changed. The change is due to television. Television, unlike all other previous media, is not a selectively used medium. Most people use television relatively non-selectively. They watch not by the program but by the clock.

Television is on an average of 7 hours a day in the typical American home. In half of our homes, typically homes that cannot afford a great variety of cultural activities, it is turned on in the morning and turned off at night. It is used as a ritual. It has become the functional equivalent of a new religion. It reaches those whom no previous central authority could reach, such as children, and reaches them at home, quickly and continuously. It incorporates most of what we know in common such as art, science, and government. It has replaced the church in that historic nexus of power which used to be state and church.

Television presents a common world to all our people, the only common denominator in an otherwise heterogeneous nation, the first true melting pot of our country. That common world is the largest single source of information. Most of it comes from entertainment. I call entertainment the education we choose for its immediate rewards.

We have studied the effects of television on our health habits, on images of science, on conceptions of medicine, on orientation to politics, on occupational choices, on educational and intelligence test scores, on violence, religion, and other issues. (Write me and I'll send you some reports.)

Now I go into my second step. What are some general features of the world of television? For the first time in history children are born into a symbolic world that does not originate with parents, church, or school, and requires no literacy. Television has replaced most stories told by parents, and has either replaced or reorganized what we learn in school or in church. It has become the norm, the standard to which we all have to relate. We use it as a measure of our own behavior and of the behavior of people around us. We use it as a way of defining ourselves. Even if you don't watch television, you get it through other people who do.

The process of presenting a common world to an otherwise heterogeneous community has for many people enormous attractions. These are people who never read books, people who never participated in the riches of culture, people who never saw anyone who was famous or powerful or beautiful or infamous, people who are isolated, parochial, removed from the centers of action. These people are now all in the mainstream. That is the enormous attraction of television. No one is out in the sticks. You can be in the hospital or in a prison, you can be very young or very old, you can be anywhere and anybody—you are now part of the mainstream. You can be very poor and still many of the same famous and rich and beautiful and ugly people come into your own home as they come into the homes of rich people.

For many this is a tremendous enrichment of cultural horizons. They will not give it up. They will not turn it off. Even to ask them is an arrogance that does not respect the genuine attraction of being a part of the mainstream to people who have always been out of it. What we should do is to ask about its dynamics, ask about its lessons, because that is not a private business. It has become a major, central, public issue and problem of our times.

Now the third step. A typical viewer of prime time sees a cast of about 300 characters each week. A very stable cast. We have been monitoring it for 18 years. What kind of cast is this? Well, about 41 characters a week are engaged in law enforcement. Protecting society is the main preoccupation of the largest single occupation on the air. Prime time is a time of power. That is why it has so much violence. (Daytime is a time of *internal turbulence*. For all its melodramatic qualities it has much more relevance to things that are close to people than the feverish macho rituals of prime time.) While 41 characters enforce the social order, about 23 criminals threaten it each week, week in and week out. There are about 12 doctors, 6 lawyers and 3 judges engaged in enforcing the rules of the game.

All-in-all, men outnumber women 3 to 1. The representation of young people (under 18) is one-third of their true proportion in the population. The representation of old people (65 and above) is less than one-fifth. These are marginal markets and thus marginal people; television unwittingly favors the world of its best customers.

The question of representation is not just a question of numbers, like a census. It is a question of the range of opportunities that people growing up in the cultures learn about. If you are white, male, in the prime of life, there are no limits. You can do almost anything. If you are a woman, non-white, young or old or in any sense some member of a minority, you are under-represented not only in number but also in opportunities, save one: You are over-victimized.

Violence is a demonstration of power. On TV it is a dramatic device to demonstrate what happens between different kinds of people in a conflict. Who tends to get away with what against whom? That is the principal lesson of violence. To reduce that to the question of aggression alone as an isolated behavior is sheer obfuscation. It is the favorite media question because, as the programs themselves, it has a repressive control function. Although true on a low level, it is not the major lesson.

The more we're exposed to violence-laden television, the more we exhibit what we call the "mean world syndrome." We absorb a sense of mistrust and insecurity, a sense of living in a mean and dangerous world in which we must protect ourselves and in which we must depend on strong people and measures for protection. If anything, it's a device that tends to put people in their place according to their status. It makes those who are lower in status feel weaker and more vulnerable and more easily controlled.

There is a direct correlation between amount of exposure and expressions of insecurity, vulnerability, and dependence. The slight, if often tragic, relationship to actual imitated violence is the fallout from this vast social control exercise. I submit that we should be equally concerned with the kind of debilitation that increases feelings of vulnerability, powerlessness, feeling of dependence, especially among those who are already more vulnerable, who are already lower on the scale of power, namely women, children, minorities. This is the mechanism that maintains and exacerbates the injustices and the inequities of our society. That is how violence really works.

Now my fourth step. One would think that in what has been called a wasteland (it's not a term I like because it doesn't give full justice to its rich dynamism) children's television would be an oasis. Unfortunately, the opposite is true. It's the real desert. It is called the "kidvid ghetto" in the industry. Like a ghetto or slum, it is the high profit, quick turnover, most exploited sector of a market.

There is no other civilized country that I know that doesn't have at least a half hour of high quality programming for children in prime time. We don't have a single network that has any kind of regular children's programming even once a week. Public broadcasting used to provide most quality children's programs. But for the first time in our television history, the fall schedule will be devoid of any original programming produced for PBS by an American producer. Instead, the schedule will be composed of foreign acquisitions and repeats.

Where do quality children's programs come from? They come from PBS and from abroad. The BBC, the Italian, French, Scandinavians, Germans, or Japanese TV systems have between four and six times the number of hours of new programming we have. Many of the highest quality programs that win international festival prizes of children's programming come from the Soviet Union and other countries of Eastern Europe. That's where you will find some of the most popular productions, the classics, the highest-paid talents, and the most compelling stories of family, friendship, and cooperation on television. Unlike our situation of not having any decent programs, the Soviet Union has several major studios engaged only in producing children's films and programs.

In the transfer of controls from partly public to mostly private hands, in the shift of controls from one set of large conglomerates to another set of even larger conglomerates, otherwise called deregulation, and under the impact of the "merger mania," the previously existing mechanisms of citizen participation and consumer protection are being dismantled. The first to suffer is always the weakest and most vulnerable. The situation is a national disgrace of world-class proportions.

Now the fifth and final step. The Wirth-Lauterberg bill, which would mandate five hours of children's programming during the week, is not censorship but its opposite; it is a step toward liberation of television from the constraints of the marketplace selling children to the greediest and highest bidder.

We need a new environmental movement, addressed at the environment that is most crucial to our humanity, the environment of stories we tell our children, the environment that shapes so much of what we think and do in common. This environmental movement has to be a coalition of parents, health professionals, educators, and citizens. It is designed not to censor but to *liberate* from the iron censorship of a market of manufactured daydreams that debilitate and hurt so many. That, at least, is a dream that heals.

READERS: AN ENDANGERED SPECIES?[1]

HARVEY C. JACOBS[2]

Addressing an audience very familiar with the problem he planned to discuss, Harvey C. Jacobs, editor of the *Indianapolis News*, told the Central States Circulation Managers' Association, "In a society saturated with communications, it is ironic that information in depth, as newspapers try to present it, is not as popular as it used to be." Pointing out that most homes and hotel and motel rooms today don't even have a spot with adequate illumination for reading, although all are equipped with television sets, Jacobs concluded, "This society is simply not attuned to newspapers, as it should be. It is not oriented toward books, as it should be. It is not a reading society, as it should be. I say this with regret, but I say it with certainty. . . ."

Jacobs organized his speech to 350 newspaper circulation executives and two other editors according to a problem-solution division. In developing his theme, the editor appealed to both the business and altruistic concerns of his audience. He told them that they should be concerned by the failure of newspapers to keep up with magazines and broadcast media in the competition for the attention of the buying public; he also argued that they have an ethical responsibility to help create an audience of literate readers. Conceding that the reasons for decreasing attention to reading are many and complex, Jacobs then outlined his solution, his promised "few thoughts on what should be done to help newspapers hold their traditional position as a growing mass medium and as the pre-eminent medium of historical record."

Harvey C. Jacobs's speech: Winston Churchill once gave this advice to public speakers: One, never walk up a wall that's leaning against you; two, never try to kiss a person who's leaning away from you; and, three, never speak to a group that knows more about the subject than you do.

You work much closer to the readers than I do.You know readers very well, I'm sure. Editors are often referred to as the ivory tower crowd, while circulation people are out in the trenches trying to peddle the product we editors and reporters create.

In recent times, however, editors have come out of their isolation and entered the real world of marketing. Editors are studying the readership surveys with the goal of making the product more marketable. They are increasingly aware of the uphill struggle to maintain circulation.

[1]Delivered as the keynote speech to the Central States Circulation Managers' Association's spring meeting at noon on March 25, 1985, in the ballroom of the Radisson Plaza Hotel, Indianapolis, Indiana.

[2]For biographical note, see Appendix.

The total circulation of daily newspapers has held its own for two decades, but it has not increased in proportion to the increase in population. Many newspapers have lost circulation, and you know what's happened to several evening newspapers. True, the total number of daily newspapers has not changed much in 40 years. And Sunday newspaper circulation has grown from 43 million right after World War II to more than 57 million. Beneath those numbers, however, there is ferment and change open to all kinds of interpretation.

For example, circulation of non-daily newspapers has doubled in 20 years. Magazines are proliferating into every specialized interest. Between 200 and 300 magazines start up every year. Into this baffling mix of printed communications we must stir in radio, cable television, regular television, videocassettes, and individual computer services. Add to the mixture dozens upon dozens of newsletters and special interest bulletins.

In short, newspapers must now compete for readers' time in a more crowded market than ever before.

Now I realize I'm not telling you anything you didn't already know, but a little background is necessary for the thoughts I want to share. My title, "Readers—An Endangered Species?" has a question mark after it. I think it's going to be tough during the next 10 years to maintain our readership in the kind of society we have created. To expand readership, as we should in a democracy, is going to be even tougher.

Two high-powered network football announcers were setting the pre-game scene before the professional players took the field. They were ticking off the names and college backgrounds of the players. One of the announcers read the name Sam Jones, then hesitated. He caught his breath, then said, "Yes, Sam attended No-ne College." There was a longer pause, after which his announcing partner interjected, "I think Sam didn't attend college at all. I think, Bill, the word after his name is 'none'."

Well, the story illustrates one type of difficulty with reading. But my concern here goes deeper. I want to sketch two broad scenes to demonstrate why readers are an endangered species, and then I'll discuss two avenues leading to possible solutions.

I grew up in a farmhouse when rural electrification was fairly new. I recall my mother's concern over the placement of the lamps. But the problem was never "how will the lamp look there?" It was: "How can the light be placed to make reading easier?" We were a family hard hit by the Great Depression, but I do not recall any budget-cutting that threatened to stop our two daily newspapers.

When Mr. Pulliam first spoke to me about being editor of *The News*, my first response was that I'd be honored to consider it because when I was growing up, two publications were always on our reading table—the *Bible* and *The Indianapolis News*. In the regular habit of reading two daily newspapers I do not think our family was much different from the dozens of other households on our motor route.

My contention is that this kind of reader loyalty does not exist much any more.

Then, take a turn through the houses of today. How many new houses—unless you enter the highest brackets—have proper illumination for easy reading? How many new houses have bookcases?

Take the average hotel or motel room. Can you find a spot in the room where you can sit down and be able to see to read a newspaper or a book? But there's always a television set, and it's properly positioned for easy viewing. And in every new home there is a family room where the set can be placed so that no viewer's vision is obstructed.

These are small quibblings, I know, but they are signs that the typical family is not oriented toward daily reading. In a society saturated with communications, it is ironic that information in depth, as newspapers try to present it, is not as popular as it used to be.

I have two sons, both relatively successful in the professional world. Both have college degrees—one a Ph.D.—and both were reared in a newspaper home, with never less than two and sometimes three or four daily papers. Eight of their growing up years were in Chicago. The *Sun-Times*, the *Tribune*, and the *Daily News* were delivered to our home every day.

Yet, these young men—yuppies, you might call them—do not subscribe to a daily newspaper. They tell me that a newspaper is not essential to their daily supply of information. I'm sorry they feel this way, but they may be more typical of their age group than we are willing to admit.

Beginning with teenagers, our newspapers try to hook young readers mostly with sports and comics. But they, and even the older age groups, say television is their primary news source and they trust it as the most accurate news medium.

This society is simply not attuned to newspapers, as it should be. It is not oriented toward books, as it should be. It is not a reading society, as it should be. I say this with regret, but I say it with certainty, in spite of the excellent sales of Sunday papers, of magazines and books. The total sales look large, but in comparison to our population they are small.

One of the reasons this is not a reading society is because the schools have not taught students how and what to read. My second point, then, deals with a shamefully illiterate society created mostly by poor schools. One in eight Americans—23 million—is functionally illiterate. That means they can spell out letters but can't fill out a driver's license or employment application without help. There's even a more alarming statistic: There are 23 million more who read and write so poorly they cannot participate successfully in a democratic society. That's 46 million persons newspapers can never reach. A new survey taken by the Library of Congress shows that nearly half of all Americans—44 percent—can read books but choose not to. They are "aliterate"—they have no will to read.

I don't mean to simply pile on the statistics, but 47 percent of black teenagers are functionally illiterate and the figure will go to 50 percent by 1990; 85 percent of all juvenile delinquents cannot read or write a simple sentence.

There is an eighth grade teacher in Indianapolis who has been giving the same kind of test to his students for 16 years, in order, he says, to try to measure how "large" the student's world is. His most recent testing involved 154 students.

Two of the 154 could not name the current president of the United States. Ninety-five could not name the vice president. Thirty-nine could not name the country in which we live. The name of our nation's capital was missed by 49 students. Nineteen could not name the state in which they lived. Twenty-nine did not know Indianapolis was the state capital. Forty could not identify Marion County as their place of residence. (Remember, these are eighth graders.)

Who are the two senators from Indiana? Would you believe that 133 out of 154 did not know. Sixty could not name the mayor of Indianapolis. Seventy-eight did not know that the Atlantic Ocean separates North America from Europe. It is incredible that 111 of the 154 did not know that Mexico is the country along our southern border.

What country did we become independent from in the Revolutionary War? Credit was given for either England or Great Britain, but 112 could not name either. Ten of the 154 eighth graders did not know how many months are in a year. Fifty-two did not know how many states are in our union.

These shocking statistics—and they represent a downward trend for 16 years—were gathered in one of our city's above-average schools. I suspect you might be equally shocked by the answers obtained in your schools.

Not long ago I received from a veteran Indianapolis high school teacher a letter with 13 misspelled words in it. A letter from another teacher began "I was shigrinned to learn . . . ."

Amid all this educational mediocrity it's fashionable to blame Johnny because he can't read or write, but I suspect he does about as well as his father or mother—or perhaps even as well as some of his teachers. Trying to assess blame for our educational problems brings back a little rhyming explanation:

The college professor says:
Such rawness in a pupil is a shame;
The high school preparation is to blame.
The high school teacher says:
Good heavens, what crudity—the boy's a fool!
The fault of course is grammar school.
The grade school teacher cries:
From such stupidity may I be spared;
They send them to me so unprepared.
The kindergarten teacher says:
Such lack of training did I never see;
What kind of woman must the mother be?
But the mother laments:
Poor helpless child—he is not to blame!
His father's folks are just the same.

The reasons for decreasing attention to reading are many and complex. There is sufficient blame to pass around. I know I have barely skimmed the surface. But I promised a few thoughts on what should be done to help newspapers hold their traditional position as a growing mass medium and as the pre-eminent medium of historical record.

First, we must do the things we are already doing, but we must do them better. I refer specifically to the Newspaper in Education program—NIE.

Newspapers used in the classroom are powerful teaching tools. Teachers who use newspapers to help teach social studies generally are enthusiastic. Students like them, too. No one really knows how to measure the circulation effect of the NIE program. We know it isn't likely to produce immediate increases but it's a wise investment in young readers. It is like water on the rock. It will take time. And it is the only way, in thousands of instances, that we can introduce newspapers into non-newspaper homes.

Newspaper publishers and their staffs must pursue other channels, too, toward becoming partners with educators. Without surrendering our right to report and criticize school systems, we must assist the educational process in every possible way. Upgrading reading and writing—for they are twins, you know—is to help ourselves. We must report more educational news—the good news, the personal news—that gives young readers a stake in our business.

Publishers and editors write a lot about mediocrity in education, but what have we done to encourage excellence? Here is a sampling of suggestions: We can endow reading workshops, give prizes to outstanding reading teachers and to students who excel in reading and writing. We can lend members of our staff for seminars and discussions. Many newspapers have generous college scholarship programs, but, in light of today's urgent reading needs, some of the scholarship funds might be diverted to in-school programs that promote reading and writing. If we don't have ideas of our own we can simply ask administrators and teachers what we can do to assist them in molding participating citizens instead of passive viewers.

We need their help if we are going to build readership among young people.

A second, and final thought—and it isn't new, either: You, we—all of us—are going to have to sell newspapers as we've never sold them before. Yes, I know you all have been selling hard. But after we've done our soul-searching and research on the editorial side, we need smashing marketing campaigns that will bring our products into 50 percent more homes than we're now reaching.

Some newspapers need to come off their elitist high horses and recognize that you sell newspapers that same way you sell soap or brushes. You go door to door, call on the telephone, do direct mail, advertise in all the media and pull out all the stops for building good will. You don't do just one or two promotional plans—you do them all. Our circulation director, Ken Todd, showed me some circulation campaign literature for *The News* from the 1920s. One of the grand prizes for champion circulation builders was the deed to a new home—a modest home, but, for the times, a good home. Another frequent prize was a new automobile. Extravagant? Inappropriate for today?

Who said so? How much is it worth to preserve a newspaper? How much is it worth to hold an audience in times when a dozen other media are beating on you? We persuade others to sell like hell—why not us?

Our traditional dignity and reticence may need to be put aside as newspapers fight for readers in a time when reading itself is in jeopardy.

We should be enlisting our personnel across the board in a brainstorming effort to make our product readable and to sell that readability to readers.

Listen to Walter Cronkite about television: "We do our job," he says, "in such a slick way that people think they are informed but they are not."

No, television is an illusion already being found out. Amid all the attention to it as background noise and babysitter, some people are becoming more selective. Some are turning away, even at this moment, to find something challenging and helpful to read.

If we are ready with a good product and if we can sell aggressively and deliver on time, we can do the job we've been doing since the founding of the republic.

"Our liberty," wrote Thomas Jefferson, "depends on freedom of the press, and that cannot be limited without being lost." I'll amend Thomas Jefferson to put it this way: Our liberty depends on freedom—and the economic success and readership—of the press, and they cannot be limited or endangered without being lost.

This, then, is the high cause we serve together: Reporters, editors, printers, mailers, distributors, salesmen and carriers. It is a powerful chain—equal, I believe, to the challenges that face us.

PUBLIC SERVICE AND PRIVATE SUPPORT

"CAN WE HELP?": PUBLIC SERVICE AND THE YOUNG[1]

DONALD KENNEDY[2]

At a time when lawmakers on Capitol Hill were urging passage of a new federal student-aid program that would provide grants to students in exchange for some type of national service, Stanford University President Donald Kennedy called for a series of national initiatives to encourage students' sense of civic responsibility. Kennedy urged his plan before 1,300 members of the American Association for Higher Education and other college and university administrators and faculty. The AAHE is an organization of administrators, students, faculty, trustees, and interested individuals who seek to clarify and help resolve critical issues in postsecondary education in public and private colleges and universities through conferences, publications, and special projects. Kennedy is one of three heads of the Project for Public Community Service, a group of more than 100 institutions interested in promoting student volunteerism. In addition to efforts on their own campuses, the presidents are working to formulate public policies that legislators could employ to promote civic involvement by students (*Chronicle of Higher Education*, March 19, 1986, p. 35).

In his speech, Kennedy addressed the claim that today's students are apathetic, conformist, self-interested, and primarily concerned with "being very well-off financially." Citing surveys which seem to support these allegations, Kennedy asked,

> Are these indicators of an innate selfishness? Have we somehow contrived, without knowing it, to spoil a whole generation of American youngsters? Or are we simply seeing some predictable responses to the messages we have been sending?

Kennedy suggested that this was an "instance of blaming the victim." Today's young people, he asserted, are reacting to "an unparalleled relative disadvantage" in U.S. society.

Basing his opinion on experience with the undergraduates of the 1980s, Kennedy argued that the critics were wrong, and that in fact "there is some surprising good news." Despite discouragement, he contended, "there is a large reservoir of social responsibility there. What it needs is some productive outlets, and some enthusiastic encouragement and approval." Kennedy then devoted the remainder of his speech to rec-

[1]Keynote address to the annual meeting of the American Association for Higher Education, International Ballroom Center, Washington Hilton Hotel, Washington, D.C., delivered at 7:45 P.M., March 12, 1986.

[2]For biographical note, see Appendix.

ommending what should be done to encourage social responsibility among young people. [Sargent Shriver, in his address on the 25th anniversary of the Peace Corps (pp. 166-75), and Franklin A. Thomas, in his speech, "Youth, Unemployment, and National Service," *Representative American Speeches, 1982-1983*, pp. 43-54, consider the same problem.]

Donald Kennedy's speech: After I agreed to do this I learned that the theme was "less talk, more action." It is a truism to say that our future is in the hands of our young people. But no truism was ever truer; and no group in this country knows its truth better than we, right here in this room—we who are privileged to have an observation point past which the best young men and women in America move, pausing long enough to allow us to watch them grow and change and begin to form the foundations of their lives and of our nation's.

The marchers in that line comprise the most important resource our society has. If we succeed with them, our national life will continue to grow and improve—and they will, incidentally, take good care of us! But if we fail, they will settle a hopeless burden on their successors, and plunge us into a cycle of deepening intergenerational debt.

Which prospect is likelier? And on whom does it depend? Is it we or they who have primary responsibility for the outcome? The answer to that, surely, is we as well as they; after all, could anyone deny that the older generation—of parents, of educators, of voters—must provide the right starting conditions, superintend the launch, set the initial course?

Yet there are signs that a troublesome mythology is arising—one that discounts the prospects for today's younger generation in advance, as though it had some inborn error of social metabolism. There is a lesion, it is asserted, in *their* sense of public responsibility. Young people are less concerned about the public interest and the welfare of their communities, and more interested in their own economic security. There are countless examples of this myth; it was already well established in 1980, when Landon Jones, in a book about the baby boom entitled *Great Expectations*, wrote of the new college generation, "What we see now is a generation coming to college that is as different from the baby boom as night from day. Today's students are passive, conformists, materialistic." Since then, the notion has only become more firmly implanted.

Even if the myth were true, I think, it would be yet another instance of blaming the victim. That is a bad habit, for two reasons. First, self-delusion is never a good idea; more important, like any other prophecy, this kind may become self-fulfilling. In the hope of helping to avert that fate, I want to spend the next few minutes talking about the kinds of economic and social prospects we have given our young people over the past decade or so, and about the signals we have sent them concerning their obligations to community. After that, I hope to address the future, with some suggestions about how we can change both the prospects we are creating, and the signals we are sending.

First let me talk about economic prospects. The generation of students that will graduate from college in the decade of the 1980s is unique in a number of respects. Caught, as it were, between the baby-boomers and the baby-boomers' children, it forms a part of the first American generation whose members will lack access to the great American dream of generational improvement. These young men and women, by and large, will not have access to the economic advantages afforded their parents. Moving one's young family into a house at a fixed, low-interest mortgage; experiencing extraordinary appreciation on land and other assets; being able to increase the probability that one's own children will receive higher education; having access to full employer-financed health benefits; being comfortable about one's retirement protection at age 40; all these opportunities were commonly available to the college graduates of our generation. But they will be available only for the very most fortunate in this one.

That is discouraging enough; but our national vital statistics tell an even more depressing story. Perhaps the most gripping one is that between 1960 and 1982, the suicide rate for 15-year-old Americans more than doubled, in a period during which suicide rates for the elderly were dropping significantly.

And that change was a response to real economic difficulties. Between 1970 and 1982, the proportion of Americans over 65 who live in poverty was reduced from 24% to 15%. But in that same period, the proportion of those under 14 living at poverty levels or below grew from 16% to 23%. Thus the positions of elderly and young Americans with respect to the most critical indicator of economic danger in this country were exactly reversed in just a dozen years.

The "juvenilization of poverty" is just as real as the "feminization of poverty." We have dramatically altered the way in which we allocate social resources to different portions of the life cycle in this country. The result is that, proportionately, the elderly are doing better, and the young much worse. In 1970, for example, about equal shares of the gross national product were spent on health and on education. A dozen years later, expenditures for health had grown half again as large as those for education. That, in itself, indicates a major proportional shift of resources from young to old, because of course health-care expenditures occur primarily at the end of life and educational expenditures mainly at the beginning. But even within the health sector, the new commitments have been heavily concentrated on such diseases of age as cancer, heart disease, and stroke. The result is that from 1968 to 1980, mortality rates for Americans between the ages of 70 and 80 were reduced about four times as much as mortality rates for the age group between 10 and 20.

For a more extended analysis of these and other data, I hope you will consult the work of Samuel Preston, a demographer at the University of Pennsylvania who has written thoughtfully on this very important phenomenon. This brief summary makes the point that we are in the midst of a sea-change in the political economy of the United States, one that is putting young people at an unparalleled relative disadvantage. It would be astonishing if they did not sense that change, and react to it. The evidence strongly suggests that they do.

Each year, as you know, the American Council on Education and UCLA conduct a massive and carefully constructed survey of college freshmen. This invaluable data base, put together by Dr. Alexander Astin and his colleagues, gives us a revealing glimpse of changes in attitudes among young people. Since 1972, there has been a conspicuous increase in the positive responses students give to values that we might call "self-interested": being well-off financially, having administrative responsibility for others, obtaining recognition. The value item with the largest growth between 1972 and 1983 was "being very well-off financially," which increased from 40% to 70%. Over the same period of time, there were declines in various values that can be thought of as community-directed: promoting racial understanding, keeping up with political affairs, cleaning up the environment, and the like.

Are these indicators of an innate selfishness? Have we somehow contrived, without knowing it, to spoil a whole generation of American youngsters? Or are we simply seeing some predictable responses to the messages we have been sending?

Let us examine the content of the messages. There is, first of all, the powerful economic signal I have just described. It is not merely that economic opportunity has been narrowed, although that is surely true. It is that, in addition, we have pursued a whole array of policies that contribute to a loss of equity between the generations. Surely that must be obvious to the loser generation. The Gramm-Rudman-Hollings legislation, which at Stanford we have taken to calling "Grambo," requires the reduction of "controllable" federal expenditures—but the government will not consider a tax increase, control military spending, or modify entitlement programs. Scholarship aid for undergraduates is slashed and subjected to ever-more-stringent tests of financial need; but Social Security and Medicare are not means-tested at all. Graduate fellowships aren't indexed to the cost of living, whereas social security payments to the retired are. How can we possibly believe that these messages aren't read and understood? How dumb do we think they are?

Thus I think that our management of the American political economy has given our young people ample reason for heightened concern about their own survival. That alone might be enough to account for a certain preoccupation with personal security: If no one else seems inclined to help you, you'd better lay plans to help yourself.

We might have reduced that reaction somewhat had we accompanied our economic policies with some high-minded rhetoric about public responsibility—preaching to them, as it were, while we lifted their wallets. But alas, we didn't even do that. Instead, there has been a steady barrage of criticism against the institutions that most centrally embody our ideas of public service and duty to community.

In one hit-and-run report on American education after another, the schools have been attacked as ineffective, and teachers for the most part as incompetent. In general, these reports have offered little by way of thoughtful remedy, and the government entities involved have been conspicuously reluctant about making any long-term commitments to improve the situation. We are left to conclude that if only there were better teachers, and more of them, and if they only offered more days of class per year and more class hours per day, the schools would do their job. I hope very much that the resulting attention of Americans to the schools will ultimately serve to bring about reform, but I worry that, in the interim, both teachers and would-be teachers have become too demoralized to give the effort the leadership it needs.

And more generally, we have seen an extraordinary wave of national hostility toward government and government institutions. That phenomenon began in earnest in the middle 1970s. Since then, candidates for major national office have vied with one another to see who can deride the civil service in the most colorful way. I speak, I must confess, with particular fervor on this subject. When I arrived to head the Food and Drug Administration early in 1977, the regulatory agencies of government had received the brunt of this new attention. After inspecting the devastation that had been wreaked on my new organization's employees, I quickly concluded that the restoration of self-respect was my primary task.

The climate has not improved much since then; bureaucracy-bashing is still a prominent element in much of national campaign rhetoric. Somehow, it does not strike most people as inconsistent when a candidate for Presidency of the United States heaps scorn on the very apparatus over which—he devoutly hopes—the voters will soon grant him control. It reminds one of the small boy who goes off to summer camp and writes home: "Dear Mom and Dad: The food here is poison—and there's so little!"

And in the classroom and in the library, today's undergraduates are likely to encounter a high degree of skepticism about the efficacy of government interventions into human welfare. The intellectual equivalent of bureaucracy-bashing along the campaign trail is the neoconservative insistence that the great social programs of the 1960s failed, and that similar interventions are similarly doomed. They don't bother to add that this conclusion is reached by the same social sciences, using the same methods, that created just the opposite orthodoxy a couple of decades ago!

Well, that is probably about enough of that. My point is straightforward enough; given the character of the messages we have been sending, why should we be surprised that college students are indicating a high level of concern for their own economic features? Do we really have a right to complain when they appear focused on self-interest? Even if they had good things to say about public service, why would they assume that their elders would want to hear them?

Well, there is some surprising good news. Despite all of these discouragements, my experience with the undergraduates of the 1980s tells me that there is a large reservoir of social responsibility there. What it needs is some productive outlets, and some enthusiastic encouragement and approval, to counterbalance the messages I have just been talking about. At Stanford and at many other colleges and universities represented in this room, campus initiatives to promote and encourage public service have been producing dramatic results—results that offer the promise of changing the depressing self-fulfilling prophesies we have been hearing about this generation from its elders.

Why have we been "pushing" public service? There are at least two good reasons. The first is that we are, after all, teachers, and that a central fact of life in this society is the symmetry between individual rights and personal freedoms on the one hand, and public obligation and responsibility on the other. John Gardner put it well at the first Stanford conference, called "You Can Make a Difference." He said, with wonderful succinctness, this: "Freedom and responsibility. Liberty and duty. That's the deal." And he went on:

> In the stable periods of history, meaning was supplied in the context of a coherent community and traditionally prescribed patterns of culture. On being born into the society you were heir to a whole warehouse full of meanings. Today you can't count on any such patrimony. You have to build meaning into your life, and you build it through your commitments—whether to your religion, to an ethical order as you conceive it, to your life's work, to loved ones, to your fellow humans. People run around searching for identity, but it isn't handed out free any more—not in this transient rootless pluralistic society. Your identity is what you've committed yourself to.

I think the notion of the social contract is being rediscovered: by sociologists (see the fascinating book *Habits of the Heart*) and even by politicians (note the thoughtful discussions of generational equity by, among others, Senators Moynihan and Durenberger). The young people in our institutions are especially fortunate, and they thus have an extra obligation as well as the extra opportunity to contribute to the public interest.

There is a second, equally compelling reason. Given all we have said to them, it is important now for us to display some confidence in the rightness of their impulses. When you ask people to do things, you show your regard for them. "We need you" also says: "We trust you, and respect you." Thus the call to public service is not simply an appeal to help society, not a request to exercise some form of *noblesse oblige*. It is an invitation to become a stakeholder in this great joint venture of ours.

What have we been doing to help? At Stanford, for example, the public service initiative began four years ago. My associate Catherine Milton undertook an assessment of opportunities for government internships, volunteering, and the like; she found that there were many, distributed around the campus, but that clear points of access were difficult to find and the level of coordination was disappointing. While her assessment was under way, a number of students joined in the effort, and their enthusiasm briskly transformed analysis into action. Part way through that first year, they sponsored a conference on Entrepreneurism in the Public Sector, and it drew large and enthusiastic audiences. Subsequently Stanford has established a Public Service Center; it includes a Volunteer Network, a program for summer and academic-year internships, supported summer and post-graduate fellowship programs, both of which received significant financial support, a public policy forum, career advising for students interested in the public and independent sector, and an annual conference that grew out of the first one.

A number of indicators suggest that we have succeeded in raising students' awareness of their obligation to help. The rate of volunteering for the Peace Corps and Volunteers in Asia has nearly tripled over the past two years. In each of the last half-dozen quarters, the Student Volunteer Network has produced over 500 Stanford students to work on various community projects on Saturdays. The Stanford-in-Government Program had 120 undergraduates in Washington last summer, and a smaller number in Sacramento; the 14 available special summer fellowships drew over 70 applications. I hasten to add that this record could be matched or exceeded at a number of institutions; the great thing about it is that it is a generalized phenomenon, not limited to any particular campus setting.

Perhaps the best evidence for this is the Project for Public Community Service, a consortium now consisting of over 100 institutions, and growing daily. This project is housed at Brown

University and operated by the Education Commission of the States. Frank Newman, who is well known to many of you, has been an invaluable godfather in getting this movement established and then disseminated; Susan Stroud and Melissa Auchard, recently a Student Body President at Stanford, are its staff officers in Providence. My colleagues Howard Swearer at Brown and Father Tim Healy at Georgetown worked with me and many other university presidents to help get it started. We may soon be talking of it as the "campus compact." Its aims are simple; to reestablish students' commitment to service for others, to help develop policies that academic leaders and educational administrators and legislators can employ to make the climate more hospitable to such service, and to develop networks that will match students seeking opportunities to local and regional needs.

If these local and national efforts succeed, then the universities will have taken leadership in a movement of extraordinary value. What we seek, and what we seem to be accomplishing, is the legitimization of some powerful but repressed impulses on the part of the best young men and women in this country. To realize and to reward the value of these impulses, and to establish status for the resulting action, will be a significant accomplishment.

But it will not do the whole job. The restoration of enthusiasm and the reinstatement of public regard can make a difference, but unless the social and economic parts of the equation change, that difference may not be enough. That takes me back to where I started: to the need for a set of national policy reforms that recognize the crucial importance of social investment in the young. That is why my title—"Can We Help?"—was meant to suggest something we ought to be saying to them, and not the other way around.

To begin on the expenditure side of the budget, what we have is a Draconian solution: a deficit-reducing, balanced-budget rule is created and the legislature has to abide by it come what may. In my judgment, any solution of that kind must have its most profound impact on those forms of current spending that have some degree of future time preference. There is no way in which we can fix the budgetary bottom line for this government without reducing the very kinds of year-by-year expenditures that have some chance of making a difference in terms of future investment. You *know* that financial aid to college students, research programs, and various kinds of expenditures for education and science facilities will be among the first to go in any system that is sensitive to the annual bottom line, and in which other kinds of policy modifications are not made.

Now let me turn to the revenue side. We are supposed to be in a period of tax reform and simplification. What bounced around in the House Ways and Means Committee and finally emerged last year is not reform any longer; it first became simplification without reform, and then neither of the above. The present version, it seems to me, manages to discourage philanthropy, discourage the use of private funds for public purposes, and withdraws important tax incentives for investment—all without doing the *one* thing that a tax proposal these days really ought to do, which is to improve revenue. We badly need to reform the tax structure, but I think we need to do so in a way that weighs education and other future investments much more heavily. If you agree, tell it before you leave town to your favorite Senator—especially your favorite member of the Finance Committee!

Most important of all, the Gramm-Rudman solution and the tax reform proposals, taken together, embody a strange paradox, by *refusing to accept a world in which we tax ourselves in order to invest in our children's future*. In short, these schemes give no opportunity at all for revenue improvement. What we really ought to be asking ourselves in this country, I think, is this: How can a society that is as productive, successful, and ambitious as ours tax itself so little? Are we really not willing to give up some things for the present in order to improve our future?

What particular policy remedies would I suggest? First, we need to question our military expenditures more critically. Second, we must explore more ways to tax consumption and to spare personal investment. Third, when we reduce government expenditures we ought to target those that have relatively lower investment value. These include some sacred cows, but we need to take them on. In particular, I hope we can stop the indexing of Social Security payments—a practice that arose as a consequence of Congressional accident anyway, and that most thoughtful welfare analysts believe was a mistake. I also believe we should consider applying means tests to *every* program of that sort; we simply cannot afford a situation in which every program you can think of—from farm subsidies through Medicare to Social Security—supports citizens without any regard to their ability to support themselves. Finally, we must support our investments in human capital by increasing expenditures for schools and for education, and also by improving our national capital infrastructure for innovation through continuing and enlarging the incentives for investment in research.

We have been described as a society hopelessly hooked on the present, and relatively indifferent to the future—as a nation of "wanters," rather than "waiters." In the test of a society's time preference, education is a key element: It is the ultimate test by which we measure our sense of responsibility for our collective future. How education will look in the 21st century depends on what we are willing to give up for it in what remains of the 20th. On the basis of our present distaste for self-denial, its quality will be nothing to make us proud; but we can change that. My main point, and I end with it, is this: The decisions we are making right now will determine a future that will be beyond the capacity of our sons, or our daughters, or our students, to retrieve and reshape.

THE PEACE CORPS: ITS HISTORY, IDEALS, PROBLEMS, AND ACCOMPLISHMENTS[1]

SARGENT SHRIVER[2]

He began his address:

> Dear friends: Let us all rejoice! Today we are gathered to commemorate a unique occasion in American history, that occasion when for the first time an American president proposed to put the full strength of our government behind a voluntary movement of free men and women dedicated to the pursuit of peace. Many nations in human history have undertaken many tasks: Many have boasted about their economic power and military victories. But none has ever put its prestige and money into so sustained an effort to seek peace through education, work, and service to others, performed by its own citizens volunteering for that service.

The occasion was the commemoration of the 25th anniversary of the founding of the Peace Corps. The speaker was Sargent Shriver, the first

[1]Delivered as part of a two-day symposium, "America's Role in Africa's Development: Past and Future," at a luncheon meeting in the banquet room of the Michigan League, University of Michigan, Ann Arbor, Michigan, 12:15 P.M., October 14, 1985.

[2]For biographical note, see Appendix.

director of the Peace Corps. And the site was the University of Michigan in Ann Arbor, where on October 14, 1960, a young candidate for the presidency of the United States, John F. Kennedy, first announced his proposal to launch the overseas volunteer service. In the quarter of a century since the program's inception, 120,000 Americans have served as volunteers in more than 90 countries around the world, assisting men and women to better the often harsh conditions of their lives.

To mark the beginning of a yearlong celebration of the 25th anniversary of the Peace Corps, the University of Michigan organized a two-day symposium, "America's Role in Africa's Development: Past and Future." Africa was chosen as the focus of the conference, according to conference chairwoman Niara Sudarkasa, "because of its overwhelming importance in today's world and because so much of the effort of the Peace Corps has been devoted to that continent." Participants in the commemoration included Vice President George Bush, current Peace Corps Director Loret Miller Ruppe, and internationally recognized experts on African economic and social developments. Shriver, brother-in-law of John F. Kennedy and the Democratic vice-presidential nominee in 1972, addressed approximately 300 symposium participants, university officials, faculty, students, Peace Corps officials and returned volunteers, and state political leaders.

Following a review of the origins and some of the accomplishments of the Peace Corps, Shriver turned his attention to the future, citing problems needing attention and proposing specific courses of action. He urged the conferees:

> Today I recommend that we remember our beginning. We are dedicated to the pursuit of peace, which means we oppose the idea that war is inevitable. We believe that with God's help we can get rid of war. We are a corps, a band of brothers and sisters, united in the conviction that if we work hard enough we truly can avoid war and achieve peace. And we all think that everyone in the Peace Corps, and everyone who has ever worked in the Peace Corps, is a special person, who, given a chance, will overcome any problem.

The University of Michigan News and Information Services reported that the audience responded enthusiastically to the speech. [For another speech on the influence of the Peace Corps, see "Tribute to John F. Kennedy," by Thomas J. Scanlon, *Representative American Speeches, 1983–1984*, pp. 153–157.]

Sargent Shriver's speech: Dear friends: Let us all rejoice!

Today we are gathered to commemorate a unique occasion in American history, that occasion when for the first time an American president proposed to put the full strength of our government behind a voluntary movement of free men and women dedicated to the pursuit of peace. Many nations in human history have undertaken many tasks; many have boasted about their economic power and military victories. But none has ever put its prestige and money into so sustained an effort to seek peace through education, work, and service to others, performed by its own citizens volunteering for that service. The success of the Peace Corps is proof that moral vision coupled with perseverance and courage can overcome great obstacles.

The road to success has not always been easy. The initial success of the Peace Corps in tapping the idealism of Americans—and sharing it with others—was overshadowed by the twin disasters of Vietnam and Watergate. Lying and vast deceptions, practiced upon our own people by persons occupying the highest positions of trust and political power, did almost crush the Peace Corps's early promise. But let us rejoice again! The Peace Corps has emerged from bureaucratic obscurity where it was buried under Richard Nixon.

Now the Peace Corps has a new mandate (passed by Congress and signed into law by President Reagan) to increase its volunteers to a minimum of 10,000. Partisan political considerations have been outlawed as factors to be weighed in the appointment of Peace Corps officials. And the current Peace Corps leadership, notably in the person of Loret Ruppe, is imaginative, dedicated, resourceful, and wise. The present state of the Peace Corps is good. Its chances for future growth and progress are better than they have been for many years.

There are certain other extraordinary realities in Peace Corps history worthy of special note today.

The Peace Corps administrative, financial, and personnel record, over 25 years, may well be the most remarkable of any government agency in this generation.

No one has ever defected from the Peace Corps! Nor has any member of the Peace Corps ever been accused of, or prosecuted for, treason. Other agencies and departments of government—even those which pride themselves on their patriotism, hard-headed machismo, and security procedures—cannot match the Peace Corps record.

No one has ever been accused of fraud or mismanagement of funds in Peace Corps history.

No one has ever been reassigned, or "fired" from leadership positions in the Peace Corps, because of deceit, lack of loyalty, personal corruption, malfeasance, or nonfeasance.

On the positive side, hundreds of Peace Corps officials and volunteers have gone onward and upward to some of the highest positions of trust and responsibility in this country. And the

Peace Corps has become the largest single source of personnel for the United States Foreign Service, for AID, for Catholic Relief Services, for CARE, and for dozens of other voluntary agencies, at home and overseas.

So, let me repeat once again: We are lucky to have been members of the Peace Corps. We are all lucky to be here, the very place where John F. Kennedy first spoke the words that led to the creation of the Peace Corps.

We are all lucky to be alive and healthy, educated and free. We are lucky to have opportunities undreamed of by nearly all the men and women who fought for and created this nation. We are lucky to have health, wealth, education, and power. And even though such gifts have often corrupted nations, even empires, we do not have to follow their examples.

Why? Because we know better. We know from history what has happened to greedy and self-indulgent nations. We cannot plead ignorance. If we do no more than follow the siren song of selfishness we would deserve to end up in the dustbin of history—just another fatuous and foolish group like those who lived in Sodom and Gomorrah or in Nineveh and Tyre. So we must not become fat, rich, smug, and self-centered.

Fortunately, we have the words and example of John F. Kennedy calling us in a different direction, appealing to us with a different vision. Listen to what he said on this campus in October 1960:

> . . . How many of you, who are going to be medical doctors, are willing to spend your days in Ghana? [How many of you who are going to be] technicians or engineers are willing to do so?
> How many of you are willing to work in the Foreign Service and spend your lives traveling around the world?
> On your willingness to do that, not merely to spend one or two years in the service, but on your willingness to spend part of your life in the service of this country will depend the answer on whether a free society can survive.

Kennedy called upon us to give our lives to service, and the Peace Corps became the instrument of his policy. "Unless you comprehend the nature of what is being asked of you," he said, "Unless you understand the nature of what is being asked of you" (I repeat it), Kennedy said, "we cannot succeed!" The Peace Corps was our answer to his words and his challenge spoken here on this campus in 1960.

The Peace Corps's nature was specifically designed to answer Kennedy's challenge. Its nature was peaceful. Its nature was to call upon all Americans to serve overseas for at least two years, and to serve at home for the rest of their lives. Service at home, according to the Peace Corps Act, involved teaching and telling our fellow Americans about the realities of the Third World with its poverty, disease, and lack of education, but also to tell us about its hopes for the future, its ambitions, its plea for help and understanding from us.

All of this is what lies behind. But what of the prospects for the Peace Corps beyond this day of celebration? It's easy and customary on an anniversary like this to reminisce, exchange old stories, and recall past triumphs. But what about the next fifteen years? Where will the Peace Corps be in the year 2000?

The time has come, I believe, for the Peace Corps to expand overseas and at home. The Peace Corps abroad should grow as Congress has authorized it to grow. Ten thousand Peace Corps volunteers abroad could be achieved by 1988; but to reach that goal, the Peace Corps budget will have to be doubled and then increased again. I use this occasion to call upon the leadership of both parties to accept that challenge and act now.

Double the Peace Corps when everything in government except the military is being cut? Isn't that a ludicrous proposal? I say "No." The cause of peace, seeking peace, is more important than any other challenge facing our country, including the military challenge. We have showered money on the Pentagon to strengthen our capacity to wage war. We have exponentially increased our power to kill. We must now increase our capacities—moral, intellectual, and political—to wage peace. First, therefore, we should increase the size of the Peace Corps overseas. Congress has authorized the expansion! The American people support the Peace Corps. Let us move forward aggressively. Let us fulfill the potential of this unique experiment in peace. Only the fainthearted would say "No."

Second. We should mobilize the returned Peace Corps volunteers here at home. Consider these facts:

We have more than 100,000 former PCVs here in America. That is ten times the number of volunteers we've ever had in any one country abroad. The PCVs worked miracles away from home. They can transform attitudes and outlooks here, too.

The Peace Corps's original, authorizing legislation, still unchanged, states that the Peace Corps and its volunteers have three objectives mandated by law. First, to supply the need overseas for trained manpower. Second, to learn more about the people, the culture, and history of foreign peoples and to teach them about the American people and our institutions. Third, to return home and educate, teach, enlighten Americans about the political, historical, cultural needs and hopes of foreign peoples and nations. The Peace Corps has done as much as it humanly could, with the resources it has had, to realize the first two objectives or purposes set forth by the Congress. But it has done precious little, almost nothing, to help or encourage returned PCVs to fulfill the third purpose of the Peace Corps legislation. The time has come to put the Peace Corps behind the pursuit of peace within the USA as well as to expand its efforts outside our own borders.

How can this be done?

Well, obviously, no one will have all the right ideas on how to carry out so challenging a mission. But there's no time to start which will be better than the present. Twenty-five years of success abroad gives reason to believe that the next twenty-five years can produce results at home as well.

Overseas, the Peace Corps has learned that it's impossible to force change. Education, example, encouragement all can help to get results. But force produces nothing but counterforce. So, the first concept we have to get rid of is the idea that we can achieve "Peace through Strength." That's a popular slogan, but it's wrong. The reverse is often true. At times, strength is best achieved through peace. Peaceful example, peaceful guidance, peaceful education, and peaceful encouragement produce results. To achieve progress it is necessary first to open hearts and minds, an objective which is not achieved by hitting, or threatening to hammer, people into submission—which seems to be the guiding principle of the government of South Africa.

So let us choose a new slogan, symbolizing a new direction—"Strength through Peace."

Second, we should utilize colleges and universities to inspire, motivate, and update our returned PCVs for peaceful service in our own land. Twenty-five years ago we called on colleges and universities to train volunteers for service abroad. Rutgers, Michigan, Notre Dame, Arizona State, Georgetown, Howard, and Harvard are just a few of the institutions where Peace Corps training began. Now we should use them to begin a new tradition of service at home.

Before 1970 only one school, Manchester College in Indiana, offered a program in Peace Studies in the whole of America! Today 35 colleges and universities offer degrees in Peace Studies, and many more offer courses, if not degree programs.

This is an extraordinary and providential development. Just when training and education for peace is essential for survival, our institutions of higher education are ready.

What do they teach?

They teach Mahatma Gandhi, Martin Luther King, Jr., Francis of Assisi, Albert Einstein, Tolstoi, Thoreau, Mother Teresa of Calcutta, Desmond Tutu, Jane Addams, Albert Schweitzer.

They teach conflict resolution; arbitration; mediation; nonviolent change; research on aggression; arms control; and international conflict resolution.

They conduct conflict management workshops for corporations like Bristol-Myers, for university personnel, for labor unions, for lawyers, and for medical doctors.

I talked with five university presidents last week and every one of them said that his or her institution is ready to inaugurate special intensive training programs in peacemaking next summer for returned PCVs. Several foundations also expressed interest. We should explore in depth their offers to help.

Next, we should support the proposals of the Coalition of Peace Corps organizations. They recommend a National Peace Corps Conference for next June; they recommend a Peace Corps Foundation to finance special projects overseas and at home; they recommend a new magazine—a "Third World Magazine"—devoted to the Peace Corps and similar activities overseas; they suggest annual awards for distinguished service by PCVs and staff members to the cause of peace.

Beyond this, we should support the idea of a universal opportunity for national service for all young people in our country. I do not mean, solely or primarily, military service. The military couldn't use all our young people anyhow. I recommend, as I have many times before, that we call upon all young persons, and that we pay them a minimum sum, to serve their fellow citizens here at home. This service should be as normal as graduation from high school. It should be an accepted part of growing up in America, a common expectation of what's expected from everyone.

This is no longer a new idea. It has been studied in depth and approved by thousands of experts. Let us now move forward with it. The VISTA volunteer program works; the National Center for Volunteer Action succeeds under George Romney's leadership; and the private sector needs volunteer help as never before.

A spirit is moving in this land—and it's not just "Cap" Weinberger's spirit. He and "Star Wars" may be dominating the headlines, but there also exists a large and growing number of Americans who, like returned Peace Corps volunteers, know more about people and the world than was ever dreamed of in Mr. Weinberger's bellicose philosophy.

The daily newspapers and TV are full of stories of violence:

In our homes: husbands and wives in unmanageable conflict; children being battered and sexually abused; adolescent runaways; elderly persons being starved.

Violence on the streets: murder, rape, assaults and battery, robbery. Never has the average citizen felt less secure, physically, than today.

Violence against our own bodies: Jane Fonda and Arnold Schwartzenegger may be leading the movement for health and physical fitness. But, excellent though their efforts are, even they cannot compete successfully against drugs, alcohol, and murder on the highways.

Violence abroad: At least three transnational wars are going on now as I talk about peace. And no one can say that within the USA we have succeeded in our struggles against drugs, against alcoholism, against racism, against militarism.

Instead of "Love your enemies" as Jesus of Nazareth taught, we are indoctrinated into "fear of our enemies." Franklin Roosevelt said, "We have nothing to fear but fear itself." He was talking about problems here at home. But his words could apply equally to our "enemies" abroad. We shall overcome communism not with bombs but with the power of the spirit, the spirit which energized Americans at the beginning of this nation. Then we talked, preached, and acted upon "The Universal Brotherhood of Mankind." We had practically no military power, but we appealed to the God-given rights of life, liberty, and the pursuit of happiness. We were popular then. Now we preach megatonnage and Star Wars, economic warfare, and boycotts. And every year we acquire more enemies.

When we started the Peace Corps, there was a big debate about the name we should give to this new venture. Many suggestions were made. "Peace Corps" was not the most popular title. Among the most experienced advisers, that title was scoffed at. They wanted a solid bureaucratic title, like The Agency for Overseas Voluntary Service.

Conservatives opposed the word "peace." They maintained it sounded soft, wishy-washy, vague, and weak. The communists, they said, had corrupted the word "peace" by applying it to every political initiative and even to every war they got involved in. Ours was also the generation of World War II and the Korean War. In our lifetimes we had never lost a war, never failed to overcome an economic depression, and never experienced Nixon, Kissinger, Vietnam, and Watergate. "Peace" was a questionable word for many of us.

The left wing disliked the word "corps." They said it sounded too militaristic. The famous German "Afrika Korps," victorious almost everywhere under General Rommel, was fresh in their minds. "Corps" sounded like a scourge.

Finally, I decided we'd use both words, put them together, and get the best out of both of them—peace because that was truly our business and corps because it showed that we were not individualists but a group.

Today I recommend that we remember our beginning. We are dedicated to the pursuit of peace, which means we oppose the idea that war is inevitable. We believe that with God's help we can get rid of war. We are a corps, a band of brothers and sisters, united in the conviction that if we work hard enough we truly can avoid war and achieve peace. And we all think that everyone in the Peace Corps, and everyone who has ever worked in the Peace Corps, is a special person, who, given a chance, will overcome any problem. In believing this about each other, in believing this about all Peace Corps people, we are giving reality to the words of Martin Luther King. He said:

Everybody can be "great" because everybody can serve.
You don't have to have a college degree to serve.
You don't have to make your subject and your verb agree to serve.
You don't have to know about Plato and Aristotle to serve.
You don't have to know Einstein's theory of relativity to serve.
You don't have to know the second theory of thermodynamics and physics to serve.
You only need a heart full of grace and soul regenerated by love.

So in 1985 we look back across a quarter of a century of grace and soul, and we know how fortunate we are. In the Peace Corps, we have known the summer heat of the Sahara, the biting cold of the Alte Plano, the endless rain of the monsoons in Asia, and the even greater obstacles caused by bureaucratic inertia.

And what a precious gift it has all been! For we have also seen the smile on the face of a child who has just learned to read; the energy of people in a dusty village who have just learned that they can lift the dead hand of hopelessness; the wondrous sense of powerless people taking destiny into their own hands for the first time. We have been pioneers of the Peace Corps world, and in that new world, we have seen the worst that happens to fellow human beings in daily acts of indifference and even evil; but we also have seen what is, what can be, the best in ourselves and in others. We have seen into our own souls, even as we have felt our eyes misting and our hearts touched when it was time to say good-bye. But for veterans of the Peace Corps enlisted in the cause of peace, whatever we do when the first tour is over, there is never a final "good-bye." We are Peace Corps volunteers forever, and we will never be the same again.

In that spirit, let us resolve to continue and complete our real tours of duty—which are not for two years, but for all the years of our lives—until the peace we dreamed of when we signed up for the Corps is finally won.

GIVING: BIG BUCKS, BARE BASICS, AND BLUE SKIES[1]

David Rockefeller[2]

"If politics makes strange bedfellows, charity makes even stranger," observed Nan Perales in the *New Orleans Times-Picayune* (October 6, 1985, p. 1). "Beginning Sunday," she noted, "the Catholic Church will pair up with the Planned Parenthood Association, Exxon Oil Corporation will side with the Student Conservation Association, and the Fresh Air Fund will meet with R. J. Reynolds Industries, the tobacco giant. They'll huddle in the halls of the Fairmont Hotel and have dinner together in the French

[1]Delivered to the annual meeting of the Independent Sector at a breakfast meeting in the Imperial Ballroom at the Fairmont Hotel, New Orleans, Louisiana, 9:10 A.M., October 7, 1985.

[2]For biographical note, see Appendix.

Quarter. They know it's weird, but they'll suffer the incongruities because they have a good cause."

Perales was reporting on the annual meeting of members of the Independent Sector, which was scheduled to begin the following day in New Orleans. The Independent Sector is an organization of some 650 corporations, foundations, and national voluntary organizations. Founded in 1980, it acts "as a meeting ground where the diverse elements in and related to the sector can comfortably come together to learn how to improve their performance and effectiveness and how to create a positive national climate for giving, volunteering, and for not-for-profit initiative." It seeks to provide "public information and education to promote active citizenship and community service and to achieve increased public awareness of giving, volunteering, and the role this sector plays in American life" (*Annual Report, 1985, The Independent Sector*, p. 18).

One of the principal speakers in the course of the Independent Sector's four-day meeting was David Rockefeller, chairman of the Rockefeller Brothers Fund. At a breakfast meeting Rockefeller addressed about 600 members of the group with a speech entitled, "Giving: Big Bucks, Bare Basics, and Blue Skies." He noted that "many recent pundits have despaired of those under 35 as only interested in themselves and material possessions." Citing recent rock concerts and records that raised large sums of money from predominantly youthful audiences for African famine relief, he concluded, "now it turns out that even yuppies may have hearts." As examples of youthful involvement in charity, Rockefeller cited Band Aid, a group of English musicians who raised $11 million with the song, "Do They Know It's Christmas?"; the song by American artists, "We Are the World," which had raised $20 million; and the daylong Live Aid concert, which raised $70 million. "Sixteen hours of rock music may be somewhat painful to members of my generation, but it certainly wasn't to those who participated," Rockefeller told the mainly middle-aged or older audience.

Although his speech was basically optimistic, Rockefeller also warned that the new momentum could falter and lead to disillusionment unless non-profit organizations become more efficient and effective. The optimism expressed by Rockefeller and others in the four days of talks was underpinned by a report to the conference that said private charitable donations reached $75 billion in 1984 and could reach $160 billion by 1990.

David Rockefeller's speech: Since my retirement from Chase Manhattan, I increasingly have found myself on the road as a "gypsy of grantsmanship"—either seeking funds for various deserving causes or promoting philanthropy in general.

In addition to many other benefits, this has proven a wonderful excuse to tour the nation. And I am sure that it will come as no surprise to you that I am especially delighted by this opportunity to be with so many friends in New Orleans—a city which is without doubt one of the crown jewels of the United States and the world.

Indeed, given the well-deserved fame of New Orleans's cuisine and night life, you all have earned credit well above and beyond the call of duty for starting such serious work so early in the day.

This timing also, of course, makes my role somewhat challenging. I am not sure exactly *why* Dick Lyman and Brian O'Connell selected me for the lead-off position. I can only surmise that they saw me either as an unfailing facilitator of further sleep, or as a new and miraculous cure for hangovers! Whatever Dick's and Brian's thinking was, they did demonstrate at least some compassion by giving me an easy task. I am supposed to respond to the question: "Can we significantly expand giving and volunteering in America?"

That doesn't take long, and my answer is simple and unequivocal: It is, *yes*, we can!

One reason for the ease of my answer is that I am preaching to the converted. It would indeed be a very sorry state of affairs if the members and friends of the Independent Sector were not already completely convinced of the important potential for philanthropic growth.

Another reason for the ease of my answer is that it is backed up increasingly by strong empirical evidence.

An especially compelling example of this evidence is the Independent Sector's own draft report on "Measurable Growth in Giving and Volunteering," prepared by a task force headed by this morning's chairman and my good friend, Ken Dayton. You all have copies of this excellent report, and it will serve as a centerpiece for much discussion during this conference. Thus, I will not attempt either to summarize it or to comment on it in detail. Three points do, however, stand out in my own mind.

First is the fact that the base is strong and the trend is positive. Individual giving in the U.S. was some $62 billion last year, up nearly 12%. Foundation giving in the same period was up 10%, to $4.4 billion. Corporate giving was almost $3.5 billion, up nearly 8%, and the corporate source of funds has grown the fastest over the past decade. Taken altogether, including bequests, private charitable giving amounted to about $75 billion in 1984—a very impressive figure!

Second is the fact that the potential for still more growth in giving is enormous. If favorable conditions continue, it is projected that giving from all sources could more than double from its

1984 level to over $160 billion in 1990. Now, in my family, at least, that's a lot of money!

Third, and perhaps most important, is the report's finding that the primary reason people give is that someone asks them. In other words, you can't expect people to give if you don't ask. And, since I believe we are only finger painters in the art of asking, this underscores the reality of the potential for significant growth.

All of these points are reinforced in a related empirical study which recently was undertaken by the Rockefeller Brothers Fund and the firm of Yankelovich, Skelly & White. This study, which will be published shortly, was based on a survey of over 1,100 adults representing a cross section of America.

It demonstrated, again, that the major reason people don't volunteer their services or give of their wherewithal is that they either just don't get around to it or simply aren't asked. The potential for growth was highlighted especially sharply by two findings. Less than 50% of those surveyed did volunteer work, yet 80% believed in volunteering. Similarly, 90% gave something, but 40% believed, in addition, that they should have given more. There also was a very strong correlation, as in the Independent Sector findings, between personal involvement and financial support. Thus, to my mind, at least, the seeds for greater giving of both time and money are definitely in place. The real question is how best to make them germinate.

For my part this morning, I would like to suggest three components which I believe are essential parts of what one might describe as a successful philanthropic greenhouse. These are: *first*, boldness in approach; *second*, rigor in application; and *third*, clarity of vision. I will focus my remarks on giving, but I am sure that many of them apply to volunteering as well—especially in view of the close interrelationship of these activities.

Too many people, I fear, view philanthropy in much the same way Victorians viewed sex—as a duty to be dutifully performed and only tainted in its moral perfection by any sense of pleasure or joy. Perhaps it's our Puritan tradition, but giving often doesn't seem "right" unless accompanied by lofty trappings of high purpose and some overtones of atonement. Boldness, the *first* greenhouse component I would like to touch upon, is rarely considered an admirable quality.

Yet something strange and unexpected is happening: More and more people are beginning to treat philanthropy as just plain fun.

Certainly Paul Newman seems to be enjoying his giving through his sales of salad dressing, popcorn, and spaghetti sauce. All of the profits from these ventures go to charity, and in the last year alone 80 different non-profit groups have received from him $1.2 million.

Or take the MacArthur awards for "genius"—no-strings-attached grants for pure talent and creativity. Some traditionalists scoffed at this concept when it was first started, but over the past 4 years 166 men and women have received $50 million just to be themselves. That, to me at least, is a very creative and joyous way to stimulate creativity.

Several months ago I attended a groundbreaking for moderate-income housing in Brooklyn. The most moving part of the ceremony was when a group of grade school youngsters joined hands and sang "We Are the World." They truly became the world for everyone there while singing a wonderful song that has raised over $20 million for famine relief in Africa.

Prior to that was the creation of the Band Aid Trust which raised some $11 million for Africa with its song, "Do They Know It's Christmas?" And, of course, the Band Aid Trust also put together the fabulously successful Live Aid Concert which raised some $70 million for the African cause.

Even more startling than the money raised was the fact that the Live Aid Concert was viewed by some 1.5 billion people in 152 nations! What was created was truly a "global village," with implications which probably will not be fully understood for years to come. In terms of philanthropy alone, it is awesome to consider the potential giving power of so many millions of people—six times the entire population of the United States. Moreover, an often tragically neglected part of the world is now the center of attention.

Sixteen hours of rock music may be somewhat painful to members of my generation, but it certainly wasn't to those who participated. If Tina Turner and Mick Jagger can have fun (and give pleasure) while raising money, why can't the rest of us?

The appeal of this type of approach can be seen in its more recent offspring. Farm Aid—the effort to help family farms in the United States—is, for instance, reported to have raised nearly

$10 million to help family farmers who may be in trouble throughout our country, and a consortium of our foremost cartoonists is developing a Thanksgiving Day world hunger forum in which virtually every cartoon will deal in some way with global hunger and solicit help for African famine relief.

It is important to note that boldness does not by any means have to be equated with brashness or boastfulness. Some of the most farsighted philanthropy today is being done anonymously in relatively small amounts. Indeed, there even is an "Incognito Fund." Other smaller family foundations are named after pet dogs and cats, and one younger acquaintance of mine even named hers "The Spunk Fund," a "spunky" synonym, of course, for boldness.

My reason for mentioning such examples is that they seem to open up a whole new vista of philanthropy which would have been inconceivable only a few years ago. They also seem to capture the spirit and energies of younger people in a way and on a scale that previously was thought impossible. Many recent pundits have despaired of those under 35 as only interested in themselves and material possessions. Such simplistic conclusions always are dangerous, and now it turns out that even Yuppies may have hearts.

Of course, all of this may be a passing fad, and it is a challenge to all of us to assure that the interest persists and grows. On the one hand, this will require that we continue to make philanthropy "new," and that we imbue it with self-regeneration so that it has the ongoing immediacy to be a source of personal joy and satisfaction. That, to me at least, is a challenge which could be a lot of fun.

On the other hand, this momentum certainly will falter if the aspirations of the donors are not fulfilled. The underlying promise is that problems of the less-fortunate will be alleviated, and failure to do so will surely lead to serious disillusionment. This brings me to the *second* essential component of the philanthropic greenhouse, *rigor in application*.

The need for better management, and greater efficiency and effectiveness, is a recurrent theme in conferences on philanthropy such as this. Often the discussion revolves around how nonprofits can benefit from the adoption of for-profit management methods. This is something like the song from the musical *My Fair Lady*, which asked, "Why can't a woman be more like a man?"

Without getting into the sexist overtones of that question for either humans or organizations, I would like to suggest that it does not go far enough. Certainly there is much that non-profits can learn from business, but it is not necessarily a one-way street. After all, many more businesses fail each year than do non-profits.

Once upon a time, as they say in children's stories, commercial banking was a relatively simple business run by solid managers trained to resist rather than to cultivate change. When I came to Chase after World War II, for instance, the bank had no human resources department, no corporate planning, no retail business as we know it today, no economic research, and very little international exposure or interest. Needless to say, it would have failed if it had remained that way. Instead, it learned to adapt to change and anticipate change. As a result, I am happy to say, it is doing quite well today.

I think that much the same challenge faces non-profits. It is mind-boggling, for example, to imagine the stolid and somewhat sober philanthropic advisors to my grandfather or my father managing a rock concert!

It seems to me that in any organization good management always depends on at least four basic qualities: clear objectives, clear means of implementation, excellent people, and flexibility. Admittedly, sometimes the importance of these attributes can be seen more clearly in their absence than in their presence.

The promoters of the effort to aid farmers, for instance, now seem to face a real quandary about what to do with the money they raised. The fact is that the plight of our nation's farmers arises from an exceedingly complex set of factors, and that there is no single easy solution to it. Thus, while helping them is unquestionably important, it is unclear at which point an application of money will have lasting impact. Motivated by a strong emotional impetus, the promoters of Farm Aid may well have gone forward before they clearly defined their objectives in terms of how to spend the money they were raising. I hope that this will be corrected, but it underscores the importance of knowing exactly what you want to do before you act.

The promoters of relief for African famine have faced a different problem. In this case, the objective is relatively clear—to put food in the mouths of starving people. The difficulty has not been in finding either the food (of which we certainly have a surplus in this country) or the hungry mouths (of which there are certainly a surplus in many other countries). It rather has been a question of effective delivery, a question of implementation. I am told that progress is being made on this score, but the delays and waste to date have cost far more than just money. They have cost thousands of lives. Even if one knows exactly what one wants to do, failure is highly probable unless the proper means of implementation are firmly in place.

Needless to say, both goal definition and project implementation demand excellent people if they are to achieve excellent results. Identifying and training such people is always a never-ending challenge, but I suspect it is particularly difficult in the non-profit sector which so often must substitute psychic for tangible compensation. Moreover, even the largest non-profit organization is small in terms of staff (though not necessarily in terms of assets) by corporate standards, and the opportunities most non-profits offer for professional growth and alternative career-pathing are usually small by comparison. In addition, the boards of many non-profits are frequently dominated by a change-resistant generation, and thus the excitement of creation and entrepreneurship is not always present. As a result, it is often too easy for them to settle for performance of a gentlemanly C or B level, rather than aiming for even the occasional A+.

Attracting excellent people demands a climate of excellence as much as it does simple compensation. Most people do not become artists or scientists or explorers or frogmen because they want to get rich. They do it because of the challenge and because of the opportunity for tangible accomplishment. It is up to the philanthropic world to do a far better job than it has been of demonstrating these qualities. If it does, it will attract more outstanding people, and excellence tends in turn to attract more excellence.

Clear goals, rigorous implementation, and first-class talent should make it relatively easy to achieve the fourth management quality I mentioned, flexibility and the ability to adapt to change. Yet, this in turn raises the question of just what changes one is to adapt to? This brings me to the *third* and final component I see in a healthy philanthropic greenhouse, *clarity of vision*.

At the beginning of this year, I made a speech on philanthropy in Ft. Worth which the Independent Sector was kind enough to distribute to its members afterwards. Some of you thus may be familiar with it, but, if not, one of my suggestions at that time was to create a type of "Nobel Prize" in philanthropy to encourage both quantity and quality.

The response to this idea has been extraordinary and, as a result, I have continued to explore it with a small group of experts in the field, including Dick Lyman from the Independent Sector. With some modifications and fine-tuning, all concerned seem to believe that the awards concept should go forward. They also have suggested, however, that any awards should be part of a larger, "think tank" type endeavor focused on the future advancement of philanthropy. They believe that more must be done to involve the vision of the best minds available from all fields to anticipate the most fruitful philosophical and practical roads to follow in philanthropy in the years ahead.

Perhaps one way of expressing the thrust of the enlarged concept is to equate it with our ability to see into space. With existing technology, we can look out some 2 million light years. With a new space telescope to be launched in connection with the passing of Halley's comet, however, it will be possible for us to see out over 2 billion light years away!

I obviously am not anticipating any such immediate leap in our capacity with respect to promoting and giving new meaning to philanthropy. Much more work has to be done to determine whether the concept of a think tank for this purpose is worthwhile, and if so, to make sure it will complement already existing related efforts. We need also to ascertain how much it will cost and who will pay for it. As you all know, none of these are simple questions! At the same time, there seems to be a deep conviction about the need for more philanthropic "blue skying" which will go beyond professionals in the field of philanthropy.

To design a program for "blue skying" in advance is in a sense to tie it to the earth before it flies. Taking my own advice, however, I will be bold enough to throw out a few possibilities.

First of all, it could be fascinating and fruitful to ask some of the world's greatest minds in science, philosophy, political science, history, psychology, sociology, and the arts for *their* opinions about what philanthropy is, what it should be, and where it is going. After all, many people in these fields benefit from private philanthropy themselves, yet I doubt if they ever really consider it within their own intellectual contexts.

A second and related task might be to gather some of the great minds in the for-profit world of marketing to explore the question of going beyond public service advertising to promote philanthropy. I hardly am an expert in this field. Indeed, my wife gave me my first color television only last Christmas—I suspect to keep me in tune with my grandchildren!

Yet I am told that most philanthropic television messages tend to appear when the fewest people are watching. Given the success of Live Aid and related efforts, this does not seem very cost-effective. What, I wonder, could be achieved if we engaged on behalf of giving the same talents which designed the campaigns for such products as Pepsi and the "new" and "classic" other brand?

Still another task might be a non-ideological review of the whole concept of aid. It is fashionable now in certain quarters of the "New Right" to view aid as an evil which actually is a cause, not a cure, of poverty, especially overseas. There may, of course, have been some cases in which this has been true. The World Bank, on the other hand, has just published an excellent review of its own programs which underscores much of the good that has been accomplished by well conceived and administered foreign assistance. At the same time, it does not gloss over problems such as irrigation projects which increase agricultural output, but also turn out to be rich breeding grounds for deadly human parasites. Wouldn't it be refreshing to have as objective as possible a review of these questions in terms which the public could understand?

Finally, it would be most useful to have an ongoing forum to explore just what we really mean by "public-private partnerships" and just what the respective roles of the public and private sectors should be under different circumstances. This is a major issue in economic development both here and abroad. I know that organizations I work with are presently struggling with this question with respect to projects such as moderate-income housing in New York and creating a new growth strategy for Latin America. And, without question, the future of private philanthropy is highly dependent on its effective relationship to the public sector. Whether we like it or not, the so-called "independent sector" is in fact highly interdependent—as we have seen graphically in the debate over tax policy in the U.S.—an area where many diverse groups share a common threat. (Glad to hear Barber Conable will be talking about this issue.)

The best questions, of course, are often the ones that one doesn't think of, and I am sure that is true in my case. Nevertheless, I would strongly suggest that questions along these general lines are basic to the future health of the philanthropic sector in which we all share an interest. They certainly have a direct bearing upon how much and how quickly we can increase giving and volunteering.

If I had to give my talk a title, it would be "Big Bucks, Bare Basics, and Blue Skies." The evidence convinces me that we already have substantial philanthropic resources at hand, as well as the potential to expand these resources dramatically. My experience has taught me that we must work very hard at planning and implementation if we are to deploy these resources with impact and excellence. Building upon past success, my instinct tells me that we must continue to dream vigorously and boldly if we are to expand the horizons of our aspirations for even greater success in the future.

None of these are easy tasks, yet none could be more rewarding. The fact that all of you are here is an especially encouraging sign that these are tasks we can and will do with both determination and style. There could be no greater gift to our children and to their children than for us to do just that.

APPENDIX

Biographical Notes

Brennan, William Joseph, Jr. (1906-). Born, Newark, New Jersey; B.S., University of Pennsylvania, Wharton School of Business, 1928; LL.B., Harvard University, 1931; honorary degrees, Suffolk University, 1956, New York University, 1957, Colgate University, 1957, Rutgers, 1958, Jewish Theological Seminary, 1964, George Washington University, 1965, Notre Dame University, 1968, Harvard University, 1968; admitted to New Jersey bar, 1931; practiced law in Newark, 1932-42, 1945-49; trial judge, New Jersey Superior Court, 1949-50; Appellate Division, 1950-52; associate justice of New Jersey Supreme Court, 1952-56; associate justice, U.S. Supreme Court, 1956- ; colonel, U.S. Army, 1942-45, Legion of Merit. (See also *Current Biography*, June 1957.)

Bumpers, Betty Flanagan (1925-). Born, Franklin County, Arkansas; Iowa State University, 1943-45; University of Arkansas, 1948-49; the Chicago Academy of Fine Arts, 1946-47; honorary Doctor of Laws degree, University of Arkansas, Little Rock, 1985; founder and president, Peace Links, 1982- ; member, Advisory Council for Immunization Policy and Practice, United States Center for Disease Control, 1983- ; trustee, National Future Homemakers of America Foundation, 1984- ; board of regents, Hendrix College, 1980- ; honorary Doctor of Humanities degree, Hendrix College, 1984; recipient of Woman of Conscience award, National Council of Women of the United States, 1985; Arkansas Audubon Society citation, 1984; Paul Harris award of the Greater Little Rock Rotary clubs, 1985; award of American Academy of Pediatrics, 1984.

Cisneros, Henry G. (1947-). Born, San Antonio, Texas; B.A., Texas A. & M. University, 1968, M.A. in Urban and Regional Planning, 1970; M.P.A. in Public Administration, John F. Kennedy School of Government, Harvard University, 1973; Ph.D. in Public Administration, George Washington University, 1975; administrative assistant, Office of the City Manager, San Antonio, Texas, May, 1968; administrative assistant to the city manager, Bryan, Texas, September, 1968; assistant director, Department of Model Cities, San Antonio, 1969; assistant to the executive vice president, National League of Cities, Washington, D.C., 1970; White House fellow, assistant to the Secretary of Health, Education, and Welfare, 1971; Ford Foundation research grantee, Harvard University; teaching assistant, Department of Urban Studies and Planning, Massachusetts Institute of Technology, 1972; assistant professor, division of Environmental Studies, University of Texas at San Antonio, 1974- ; member, San Antonio city council, 1975-81; mayor of San Antonio, 1981- ; trustee, City Water Board, City Public Service Board, 1981- ; selected "Outstanding Young Man of San Antonio," Jaycees, 1976; one of "Five Outstanding Young Texans," Texas Jaycees, 1976; one of "Ten

Outstanding Young Men of America," U.S. Jaycees, 1982; awards, Torch of Liberty Award, Anti-Defamation League of B'nai B'rith, 1982, Jefferson Award, American Institute for Public Service, 1982; member, President's Federalism Council, United San Antonio, National Council for Urban Economic Development, Governor's Council of Mayors, Council on Foreign Relations of New York, Police Foundation of Washington, D.C., Texas Municipal League, Philosophical Society of Texas.

CLARK, ALLAN HERSH (1935-). Born, Cincinnati, Ohio; B.S., Massachusetts Institute of Technology, 1957; M.A., Princeton University, 1959, Ph.D., 1961; instructor, Brown University, 1961-63, assistant professor of mathematics, 1963-66, associate professor, 1966-70, professor, 1970-75, chairman of the department of mathematics, 1971-73; professor and dean of the School of Science, Purdue University, 1973-85; president, Clarkson University, 1985- ; visiting member of Institute for Advanced Study, 1965-66; guest professor, Aarhus University, Denmark, 1970-71; author, *Elements of Abstract Algebra*, 1971.

CSORBA, LASZLO (LES) THOMAS (1963-). Born, Edmonton, Alberta, Canada; B.A., University of California at Davis, 1985; editor, *Davis Dossier*; executive council and president, student body, University of California at Davis, 1983; vice president, University of California at Davis Model United Nations, 1983; delegate, New York City Model United Nations, 1983; organizer, Davis, California "It's OK Not to Drink"; press aide, United States Senator, 1984; executive director, Accuracy in Academia, 1985- ; executive editor, *The Campus Report*, 1985- ; research fellow, Council for Inter-American Security, 1985- ; member, Sigma Alpha Epsilon, 1982- ; California director, Students for a Better America; student government service award, University of California at Davis, 1983, distinguished senior, 1985; Capitol Hill Exchange Club Speaking Award, 1986; author of several articles appearing in *USA Today*, *Human Events*, *New Guard*, *Prospect Magazine*, campus publications; one of four student journalists selected by the Council for Inter-American Security to tour Central America, 1984.

CUOMO, MARIO MATTHEW (1932-). Born, Queens County, New York; B.A., St. John's College, 1953; L.L.B., St. John's University, 1956; admitted to New York bar, 1956, U.S. Supreme Court bar, 1960; confidential legal assistant to judge New York State Court of Appeals, 1956-58; associate firm Corner, Wiesbrod, Froeb and Charles, Brooklyn, 1958-63, partner 1963-75; secretary of state State of New York, 1975-79; lieutenant governor, 1979-82, governor, 1983- ; faculty, St. John's University School of law, 1963-73; counsel to community groups including Corona Homeowners, 1966-72; charter member 1st Ecumenical Community of Christians and Jews for Brooklyn and Queens, 1965; member, ABA, New York State, Brooklyn, Nassau, and Queens County bar associations, Association Bar City New York, American Judicature Society, St. John's University Alumni Federation (chairman, board, 1970-72), Catholic Lawyers Guild of Queens County (president, 1966-67), Skull and Circle; recipient, Rapalla award Columbia Lawyers Association, 1976, Dante medal Italian Government-American Association of Teachers of Italian, 1975, silver medallion Columbia Coalition, 1976, Public Administrator award C. W.

Post College, 1977; author, *Forest Hills Diary: The Crisis of Low-Income Housing*, 1974, *Diaries of Mario M. Cuomo: The Campaign for Governor*, 1984; contributor of articles to legal publications. (See also *Current Biography*, August 1983.)

GERBNER, GEORGE (1919-). Born, Budapest, Hungary; B.A., University of California at Berkeley, 1943; M.S., University of Southern California, 1951, Ph.D., 1955; L.H.D., LaSalle College, 1980; served with United States Army, 1st Lieutenant, 1943-46; reporter, assistant financial editor, The Chronicle, San Francisco, 1942-43; free-lance publicity, 1947-48; instructor, Pasadena Junior College, 1948-51; instructor, El Camino College, 1951-56; assistant professor, associate professor, University of Illinois-Urbana, 1956-64; professor, dean, Annenberg School of Communications, University of Pennsylvania, 1964- ; grantee, United States Office of Education, 1959; National Science Foundation, 1962, 1980; National Institute of Mental Health, 1958, 1971- ; International Sociological Association, 1963; United Nations Educational, Scientific, and Cultural Organization, 1963; National Commission on Causes and Prevention of Violence, 1969; Surgeon General's Science Advisory Committee, 1970; White House Office Telecommunications Policy, 1977; United States Administration on Aging, 1978; American Medical Association, 1979; member, International Communication Association, American Sociological Association, International Association for Mass Communication Research, Association for Education in Journalism; author, numerous books and articles; editor, *Journal of Communication*, 1974- ; naturalized United States citizen, 1944.

JACOBS, HARVEY COLLINS (1915-). Born, Trafalgar, Indiana; A.B., Franklin College (Indiana), 1938; M.A., Indiana University, 1949; Litt.D., Sussex College, 1973; Litt.D., Franklin College, 1974; reporter, editorial writer, and columnist, *Franklin Evening Star*, 1937-44; director of public relations, Franklin College, 1941-49; head, department of journalism, 1949-55; assistant editor, *Rotarian*, 1955-56; head, program division of Rotary International, 1956-58, undersecretary, 1958-63; founder and chairman, department of journalism and mass communications, New Mexico State University, Las Cruces, 1963-74; director, Central Broadcasting and International Communications, 1970-74; editor, *Indianapolis News*, 1974; member, Association for Education in Journalism, American Society of Newspaper Editors, Authors Guild, Associated Press Managing Editors Association, National Conference of Editorial Writers, Indiana Historical Society, Indianapolis Press Club, Sigma Delta Chi; recipient, Distinguished Alumnus citation, Franklin College, 1957, National Headliner award, University of Oklahoma, 1970, Distinguished Service award, New Mexico Broadcasters Association, 1971, Carl Towley award, Journalism Education Association, 1974, Golden Crown award, Columbia University, 1975, Community Service award, Hoosier Press Association, 1976, Best Columnist award, 1976; fellow, Public Relations Society of America; author, *Rotary: 50 Years of Service*, 1955, *Seven Paths to Peace*, 1959, *Adventure in Service*, 1961, *We Came Rejoicing*, 1968; contributor of articles.

JORDAN, VERNON E., JR. (1935-). Born, Atlanta, Georgia; B.A., DePauw University, 1957; first prize, Indiana Interstate Oratorical Contest, sophomore year; J.D., Howard University, 1960; honorary degrees from thirty institutions; circuit vice president of American Law Students Association while at Howard University; helped to desegregate the University of Georgia; clerk in law office of civil rights attorney Donald Hollowell; field secretary, NAACP, Georgia branch, 1952; set up law partnership in Arkansas with another civil rights lawyer, Wiley A. Barnton, 1964; director, Voter Education Project for the Southern Regional Council, 1964-68; executive director, United Negro College Fund, 1970-72; director, National Urban League, January 1972-81; partner, Atkin, Gump, Strauss, Hauer and Feld law firm, Washington, D.C., 1981- ; member, Arkansas and Georgia bar associations, U.S. Supreme Court bar, American Bar Association, Common Cause, Rockefeller Foundation, Twentieth Century Fund, other service organizations; has held fellowships at Harvard University's Institute of Politics, the John F. Kennedy School of Government, and the Metropolitan Applied Research Center; serves on boards of several corporations. (See also *Current Biography*, February 1972.)

KENNEDY, DONALD (1931-). Born, New York City; B.A., Harvard University, 1952, M.A., Ph.D., 1956; faculty member, Syracuse University, 1956-60; faculty member, Stanford University, 1960-77, professor of biological sciences, 1965-77, chairman of the department, 1965-72; senior consultant, Office of Scientific and Technological Policy, Executive Office of the President, 1976; commissioner, Federal Drug Administration, 1977-79; vice president and provost, Stanford University, 1979-80, president, 1980- ; board of overseers, Harvard University, 1970-76; fellow, American Academy of Arts and Sciences; member, National Academy of Sciences, American Physiology Society, Society of General Physiologists, American Society of Zoologists, Society of Experimental Biology (U.K.); author (with W. H. Telfer), *The Biology of Organisms*, 1965; editor, *The Living Cell*, 1966, *From Cell to Organism*, 1967; editorial board, *Journal of Experimental Zoology*, 1965-71, *Journal of Comparative Physiology*, 1965-76, *Journal of Neurophysiology*, 1969-75, *Science*, 1973-77.

MALOTT, ROBERT HARVEY (1926-). Born, Boston, Massachusetts; A.B., Kansas University, 1948; M.B.A., Harvard University, 1950; postgraduate work, New York University Law School, 1953-55; served with United States Naval Reserve, 1944-46; assistant to dean, Harvard Graduate School—Business Administration, 1950-52; FMC Corporation, 1952- , assistant to executive vice president, chemicals division, New York City, 1952-55, controller, Niagra Chemical division, Middleport, New York, 1955-59, controller, organic chemicals division, New York City, 1959-62, assistant division manager, 1962-63, division manager, 1963-65, vice president and manager film operations division, American Viscose division, 1966-67, executive vice president and member of the president's office, 1967-70, manager, machinery divisions, Chicago, 1970-72, president and chief executive officer, 1972- , chairman, 1973; board of directors, FMC Corporation, Standard Oil of Indiana, Bell & Howell, Continental Illinois Corporation, Continental Illinois Bank, United Technologies Corporation; trustee, University of Kansas Endowment Association, University of Chicago, Chicago Orchestral Association; member, Chemical Manufacturers Association, Machinery and Allied Products Institute (executive committee), Business Council, Business Roundtable, United States Chamber of Commerce, Phi Beta Kappa, Beta Theta Pi, Alpha Chi Sigma.

MANATT, CHARLES TAYLOR (1936-). Born, Chicago, Illinois; B.S., Iowa State University, 1958; J.D., George Washington University, 1962; admitted to California bar, 1962; served with United States Army; legislative assistant to congressman, 1959-60; law practice, Los Angeles, 1962-63, Beverly Hills, 1963-64, Van Nuys and Los Angeles, 1964- ; partner, Manatt, Phelps, Rothenberg & Tunney, Los Angeles; chairman, Democratic National Committee, 1981- ; chairman, board of directors, First Los Angeles National Bank; executive secretary, Young Democratic Clubs of America, 1961-62; chairman, Young Citizens for Johnson, southern California, 1964, California Democratic Committee, 1971-73, 1975-77; deputy director J. V. Tunney for Senator campaign, 1970; member, Democratic National Committee, 1976- , chairman, national finance council, 1978; member, Democratic Executive Committee, 1976- ; chairman, Western States Conference, 1972-76; member, California Bar Association, San Fernando Valley Bar Association, Federal Bar Association, American Bar Association.

MEESE, EDWIN, III (1931-). Born, Oakland, California; A.B., Yale University, 1953; J.D., University of California at Berkeley, 1958; served with United States Army; deputy district attorney, Alemeda County, California, 1958-66; secretary on clemency and extradition to Governor Reagan, California, 1966-70; executive assistant, chief of staff to Governor Reagan, 1970-74; vice president, Rohr Industries, 1975-76; private law practice, 1977; director, Center for Criminal Justice Policy and Management, University of California, San Diego Law School, 1977-78, professor, law, 1978-80; advisor, Reagan presidential campaign, 1980; counselor to President Reagan, 1981- .

MURPHY, JOSEPH S. (1933-). Born, Newark, New Jersey; A.B., Olivet College (Michigan), 1955; Graham Kenan fellow, Woodrow Wilson fellow, University of North Carolina, 1955-56; M.A., Brandeis University, 1959, Ph.D., 1961; teaching fellow, instructor, assistant professor, 1957-65; director, Peace Corps Training Center, St. Croix, 1965-66; assistant secretary, Department of Health, Education, and Welfare, 1966-67; associate director, Job Corps, 1967-68; director, United States Peace Corps, Ethiopia, 1968-70; vice chancellor for higher education, New Jersey, 1970-71; president, Queens College, professor, political science, graduate faculty, City University of New York, 1971-77; president, Bennington College, 1977- ; chancellor, City University of New York, 1982- ; consultant, Virgin Islands Economic Opportunity Program, 1965-66; member, Scholarship Commission of New Jersey, 1970-71; Governor's Task Force on Transition, 1974; chairman, City Council President's Commission on Adult Education, 1974- ; member, Governor's Task Force on Higher Education, 1975; president, College Publishing Agency Council, New York City, 1973-74; member, board of directors of Queens Speech and Hearing Service Center, Queens Symphony Orchestra, New York City Chapter of American Red Cross, Ralph Bunche Institute on the United Nations, Operation Sail, Bicentennial Celebration, 1975-76; trustee, Queens County Art and Culture Center; vice chairman, regents Regional Coordinating Council for Post Secondary Education in New York City, 1973-75; author, *The Theory of Universals in Eighteenth Century British Empiricism*, 1961, *Political Theory: A Conceptual Analysis*, 1968; contributor of articles to professional journals.

NISBET, ROBERT A. (1913-). Born, Los Angeles, California; A.B., University of California, 1936, M.A., 1937, Ph.D. 1939; L.H.D., Hofstra University, 1974; instructor, University of California, Berkeley, 1939-43, assistant dean, College of Letters and Science, 1942-43, 1946, assistant professor of social institutions 1943-48, associate professor of sociology, 1948-52; professor of sociology, University of California, Riverside, 1953-72, vice chancellor, 1960-63, dean of College of Letters and Sciences, 1953-63; visiting professor, Columbia University, 1949, Albert Schweitzer professor, 1974-78, emeritus, 1978- ; resident scholar, American Enterprise Institute, 1978- ; professor of history and sociology, University of Arizona, 1972-74; visiting professor, University of Bologna, Italy, 1956-57; Guggenheim fellow, 1963-64; research professor, Smith College, 1971-72; visiting fellow, Princeton University, 1963-64; Johns Hopkins University Centennial scholar, 1975-76; served with the United States Army, 1943-45; decorated cavaliere ufficiale Order of Merit (Italy); author, *The Question for Community*, 1953, *Human Relations in Administration*, 1956, *Emile Durkheim*, 1965, *The Sociological Tradition*, 1966, *Tradition and Revolt*, 1968, *Social Change and History*, 1969, *The Social Bond*, 1970, *The Degradation of the Academic Degree*, 1971, *The Social Philosophers*, 1973, *The Sociology of Emile Durkheim*, 1974, *Twilight of Authority*, 1975, *Sociology as an Art Form*, 1976, *History of the Idea of Progress*, 1980; co-editor, *Contemporary Social Problems*, 1961, 1966, 1971, 1976, *History of Sociological Analysis*, 1978.

REAGAN, RONALD WILSON (1911-). Born, Tampico, Illinois; B.A., Eureka College (Illinois), 1932; sports announcer, radio station WHO, Des Moines, Iowa, 1932-37; motion picture and television actor, 1937-1966; program supervisor, General Electric Theater; president, Screen Actors Guild, 1947-52, 1959; captain, U.S. Air Force, 1942-45; governor, California, 1967-74; unsuccessful candidate for Republican presidential nomination, 1976; U.S. President, 1980- ; author, *Where's the Rest of Me*, 1965 (reprint 1981 as *My Early Life*), *Abortion and the Conscience of the Nation*, 1984. (See also *Current Biography*, February 1967 and November 1982.)

ROCKEFELLER, DAVID (1915-). Born, New York, New York; B.S., Harvard University, 1936; Ph.D., University of Chicago, 1940; LL.D., Columbia University, 1954; LL.D., Boudoin College, 1958; LL.D., Jewish Theological Seminary, 1958; LL.D., Williams College, 1966; LL.D., Wagner College, 1967; LL.D., Harvard University, 1969; LL.D., Pace College, 1970; LL.D., St. John's University, 1971; LL.D., University of Liberia, 1979; served with United States Army, captain, 1942-46; secretary to mayor, New York City, 1940-41; assistant regional director, Office of Defense, Health and Welfare Services, 1941-42; second vice president, Chase National Bank, 1948-49, vice president, 1949-51, senior vice president, 1951-55; executive vice president, Chase Manhattan Bank, 1955-57, vice chairman of the board, 1957-61, president and chairman of the executive committee, 1961-69, chief executive officer, 1969-80, chairman, international advisory committee, 1981- ; chairman of the board, Rockefeller Center, Inc.; member, executive committee, Downtown Lower Manhattan Association, 1958- , chairman, 1958-75; trustee, chairman of the board, Rockefeller University, 1950-75, chairman, executive committee, 1975- ; chairman and trustee, Rockefeller Brothers Fund; honorary trustee, Rockefeller Family Fund; life trustee, University of Chicago; trustee and vice chairman of the executive committee, Museum of Modern Art; member, board of overseers, Harvard College, 1954-60, 1962-68, 1973-74; Legion of Honor (France); Order of Merit (Italy); recipient, Award of Merit, New York Chapter American Institute of Architects, 1965, Medal of Honor for City Planning, New York City, 1968, Charles Evans Hughes award, National Conference of Christians and Jews, 1974; author, *Unused Resources and Economic Waste*, 1940, *Creative Management in Banking*, 1964.

SHRIVER, ROBERT SARGENT, JR. (1915-). Born, Westminister, Maryland; B.A., Yale University, *cum laude*, 1938, LL.B., 1941; LL.D., St. Procopius College, 1959, Notre Dame University, 1959, DePaul University, 1959, Seton Hall College, 1959, St. Louis University, 1961, Kansas State University, 1961, Brandeis University, 1961, St. Michael's College, 1962, Fordham University, 1962, Boston College, 1962, Yale University, 1962, Duquesne University, 1962, New York University, 1962, Wesleyan University, 1962; D.C.L., University of Liberia, 1963; H.H.D., Satem College, 1963, Bowling Green University, 1963; L.H.D., Springfield College, 1963, University of Scranton, 1963, Providence College, 1963; Dr. Polit. Sci., Chulalongkorn University (Thailand); served, United States Naval Reserve, lieutenant commander, 1940-45; admitted to New York bar, 1941, Illinois bar, 1959, United States Supreme Court bar, 1969, District of Columbia bar, 1971; law practice, Winthrop, Stimson, Putnam & Roberts, 1940-41; assistant editor, *Newsweek*, 1945-46; associate, Joseph P. Kennedy Enterprises, 1947-48; assistant general manager, Merchandise Mart (Chicago), 1948-61; director, Peace Corps, 1961-66; director, Office for Economic Opportunity, 1964-68; United States Ambassador to France, 1968-70; special assistant to the President, 1965-68; senior partner, Fried, Frank, Harris, Shriver & Jacobson, 1971- ; Democratic vice presidential nominee, 1972, presidential candidate, 1976; American Committee on East-West Accord, 1978- ; Americans for SALT, 1979- ; president, Chicago Board of Education, 1955-60; member-at-large, National Council of the Boy Scouts of America; president, Catholic Interracial Council of Chicago, 1955-60; chairman, International Organization of Patrons of Israel Museum, 1972-75; member, Yale University Law School Association (executive committee), Navy League, Chicago Council on Foreign Relations (director), Delta Kappa Epsilon; Yale University medal, 1957; Chicago medal of Merit, 1957; James J. Hoey award by the Catholic Interracial Council of New York, 1958; Lay Churchman of the Year by Religious Heritage of America, 1963; Golden Heart Presidential Award (Philippines), 1964; Laetare medal by University of Notre Dame, 1968; author, *Point of the Lance*, 1964; extensive world travel to visit Peace Corps projects, 1961-66.

SMEAL, ELEANOR CUTRI (1939-). Born, Ashtabula, Ohio; B.A., Duke University, 1961; M.A., University of Florida, 1963; member, board of League of Women Voters, Upper St. Clair (Pennsylvania) chapter, 1968-72; secretary-treasurer, Allegheny County Council, 1971-72; member, National Organization for Women, 1971- , convenor and first president, South Hill (Pennsylvania) chapter, 1971-73, president and state coordinator for Pennsylvania, 1972-75, national board of directors, 1973-75, chairwoman of the board, 1975-77, president, 1977-83, 1985- , Legal Defense and Education Fund, 1975- ; chairwoman, ERA Strike Force, 1977- ; member, first nominating committee, foundation conference for National Women's Political Caucus, 1971; board of directors, Allegheny County Women's Political Caucus, 1971-72; member, National Commission for Observance of International Women's Year, 1977, executive committee Leadership Conference on Civil Rights, 1979- , National Advisory Committee on Women, 1978; named One of the Twenty-Five Most Influential Women in the United States, *World Almanac*, 1978.

CUMULATIVE SPEAKER INDEX

1980-1986

A cumulative author index to the volumes of *Representative American Speeches* for the years 1937-1938 through 1959-1960 appears in the 1959-1960 volume, for the years 1960-1961 through 1969-1970 in the 1969-1970 volume, and for 1970-1971 through 1979-1980, in the 1979-1980 volume.